MEMORY MAKERS

Family & Friends
Scrapbook Pages

MEMORY MAKERS BOOKS

contents

family and friends scrapbook pages

6

58

76

complete index

Turn to page 4 for a complete index of ideas in this book! ➤

Executive Editor Deborah Mock

Art Director Mark Lewis

Associate Editor Darlene D'Agostino

Craft Editor Kari Hansen-Daffin

Departments Editor Trisha McCarty-Luedke

Editorial Assistant Sarah Kelly

Senior Graphic Designer Dawn Knutson

Photographer Ken Trujillo

Idea Editor Shawna Rendon

Idea Coordinator Lynda Meisner

Editorial Support Dena Twinem

F+W Publications, Inc.

Chairman William F. Reilly

President Stephen J. Kent

Executive Vice President & CFO Mark F. Arnett

F+W Publications, Inc. Magazine Division

President William R. Reed

Vice President Consumer Marketing Susan Dubois

Director of Business Planning & Analysis Matt Friedersdorf

Publication Production Manager Vicki Whitford

Contributors

Contributing Writers Heather Eades, Julie Labuszewski

Contributing Designers Jeff Norgord, Melanie Warner

Contributing Photographers Brenda Martinez, Jennifer Reeves

2005 Memory Makers Masters Jessie Baldwin, Jenn Brookover, Christine Brown, Sheila Doherty, Jodi Heinen, Jeniece Higgins, Nic Howard, Julie Johnson, Shannon Taylor, Samantha Walker

Special Thanks

We would like to thank all contributors to this book, including those participants whose pages we requested but were not able to feature because of space limitations. We appreciate your willingness to share your ideas—you are what makes this magazine unique.

The material in this book appeared in the previously published Volume 10, No. 51 issue of *Memory Makers*, a division of F+W Publications, Inc., and appears here by permission of the contributors.

Published by Memory Makers Books, an imprint of F+W Publications, Inc.
12365 Huron Street, Suite 500, Denver, CO 80234
Phone 1-800-254-9124

First edition. Printed in the United States of America.

09 08 07 06 05   5 4 3 2 1

A catalog record for this book is available from the Library of Congress at <http://catalog.loc.gov>.

ISBN 1-892127-69-5

Distributed in Canada by Fraser Direct
100 Armstrong Avenue
Georgetown, ON, Canada L7G 5S4
Tel: (905) 877-4411

Distributed in the U.K. and Europe by David & Charles
Brunel House, Newton Abbot, Devon,
TQ12 4PU, England
Tel: (+44) 1626 323200, Fax: (+44) 1626 323319
Email: mail@davidandcharles.co.uk

Distributed in Australia by Capricorn Link
P.O. Box 704, S. Windsor, NSW 2756 Australia
Tel: (02) 4577-3555

Memory Makers Books is the home of *Memory Makers*, the scrapbook magazine dedicated to educating and inspiring scrapbookers. *Memory Makers* features the ideas and stories of our readers around the world—people who believe in keeping scrapbooks and the tradition of the family photo historian alive. *Memory Makers* is committed to providing ideas and inspiration for this worldwide community of scrapbookers. To subscribe, or for more information, call 1-800-366-6465.

Visit us on the Internet at www.memorymakersmagazine.com.

fw
F+W PUBLICATIONS, INC.

book index

an index of scrapbook page ideas, products and techniques featured in this book

Create & Trade Album, p. 94

Heart & Soul, p. 60

featured scrapbookers

Meet the scrapbookers whose ideas are featured in this book. Each of these contributors receives a gift box containing scrapbook supplies generously donated by leading scrapbook-product manufacturers.

Alabama
Vanessa Hudson – Mt. Olive
Misty Posey – Decatur

Arizona
Kimberly Kesti – Phoenix
Shelly Umbanhowar – Phoenix

California
Miki Benedict – Modesto
Tracy Weinzapfel Burgos – Ramona
Diana Hudson – Bakersfield
Pamela James – Ventura
Sherry Laffoon – Modesto
Kathy Lewis – Temple City
Kathy Montgomery – Rocklin
Tamara Morrison – Trabuco Canyon
Suzy Plantamura – Laguna Niguel
Michelle Tornay – Newark
Shannon Watt – Newhall
Suzy West – Fremont
Stacy Yoder – Yucaipa

Colorado
Michelle Pendleton – Colorado Springs

Florida
Jennifer Bertsch – Tallahassee
Kristi Mangan – West Palm Beach

Georgia
Melissa Boyd – Douglasville
Kitty Foster – Snellville
Jennifer Gallacher – Savannah
Alecia Grimm – Atlanta
Sharon Laakkonen – Savannah
Danielle Thompson – Tucker

Idaho
Teri Anderson – Idaho Falls
M Sheila Doherty – Coeur d'Alene
Lorinda King – Rigby
Audrey Lewis – Meridian

Illinois
M Jeniece Higgins – Lake Forest
Donna Leslie – Tinley Park
Tara Pollard Pakosta – Libertyville

Indiana
Jen Nichols – Orland
Denise Tucker – Versailles

Kentucky
Shannon Zickel – Louisville

Louisiana
Kelly Surace – Baton Rouge

Maryland
Laura Kurz – Gambrills
Tracy Miller – Fallston

Massachusetts
Carrie O'Donnell – Newbury

Michigan
Tarri Botwinski – Grand Rapids
Jennifer Bourgeault – Macomb Township
Melissa Diekema – Grand Rapids
Melodee Langworthy – Rockford

Minnesota
M Christine Brown – Hanover
Sam Cole – Stillwater
Laurel Gervitz – Maple Grove
M Jodi Heinen – Sartell
Pamela Rawn – Champlin

Mississippi
Pam Easley – Bentonia
Jlyne Hanback – Biloxi
Angelia Wigginton – Belmont

Montana
Pam Weisenburger – Seeley Lake

Nevada
M Jessie Baldwin – Las Vegas
Leah LaMontagne – Las Vegas

New Hampshire
Robyn Lantz – Charlestown

New Jersey
Breanne Crawford – Scotch Plains

New York
Saralyn Berkowitz – Long Beach
Amy Goldstein – Kent Lakes

North Carolina
Joanna Bolick – Fletcher
Ginger McSwain – Cary

Ohio
Amy L. Barrett-Arthur – Liberty Township
Barb Hogan – Cincinnati
Cheryl Manz – Paulding
Debby Shelton – Painesville

Oklahoma
Susan Cyrus – Broken Arrow

Oregon
Shannon Brown – St. Helens

Pennsylvania
Jackie Siperko – Dallas
Denine Zielinski – Nanticoke

Tennessee
Brandi Barnes – Kelso
Doris Sander – Hermitage
M Shannon Taylor – Bristol

Texas
M Jenn Brookover – San Antonio
Carrie Colbert – The Woodlands
Angie Head – Friendswood
M Julie Johnson – Seabrook
Donna Pittard – Kingwood
Melissa Smith – North Richland Hills
Amy Warren – Tyler

Utah
Cynthia Coulon – Springville
Julie Medieros – South Jordan
Emily Van Natter – Provo

Virginia
Wendy Inman – Virginia Beach
Deb Perry – Newport News
Tina Powell – Sutherland
Traci Turchin – Hampton

Washington
Angela Marvel – Puyallap
Tenika Morrison – Puyallap
M Samantha Walker – Battle Ground

International

Canada
Tina Barriscale – Nepean, Ontario
Kimberley Kett – St. Catharines, Ontario
Cari Locken – Edmonton, Alberta
Carolyn Peeler – Langley, British Columbia
Shelley Rankin – Fredericton, New Brunswick

New Zealand
M Nic Howard – Pukekohe, South Auckland

M This logo denotes a current *Memory Makers* Master.

send us your ideas | featured scrapbookers

Perfect Love, p. 40

The only perfect thing is love.

AleX & PopPop

When the road looks rough ahead

And your miles and miles from your nice warm bed

Just remember what your old pal said...

You've Got A Friend In Me!

Sean age 4
Ben age 2

You've Got a Friend in Me, p. 86

Before you were even on earth, and you were just a dream for our future, we knew we would love you someday.

When you were becoming a part of our lives, yet still tucked away in Mommy's belly we were beginning to love you, but you had no idea.

When we first laid our eyes upon you one late, extraordinary evening, our love for you was immeasurable, but you didn't even realize what was going on.

As you grew each day, so did our love for you, even if you didn't know it.

And now you are old enough to recognize love. You know what love feels like, you know it is in our arms, in our home, in our words, our touch. You know it comes from us every day. And now you do not only receive, you give. We are loved back, in return.

You know exactly what we mean when we say "We Love You". Our love for you has been here from the start... and Ethan, it always will. You've become our greatest love, priority, and joy on earth. We are blessed that you think of us the same. -- Mommy & Daddy 4/3/2004

Family Gallery

A collection of ideas honoring parents, siblings and those we are closest to.

Love Story

Leah LaMontagne, Las Vegas, Nevada

Love given and returned is the focus of Leah's page, illustrating the amazing love exchanged between parents and child. Leah used a tripod and remote to capture this tender pose, and used a rub-on as a whimsical love note across the image of her son's back. Machine stitching, stamping inks and embossing powder add warmth and shimmer to the layout, while metal accents give a sense of permanence and strength.

---

supplies: Light blue and sage papers • Patterned papers (Creative Imaginations, Chatterbox and 7 Gypsies) • Rub-on letters (Making Memories) • Ribbon (Offray) • Bronze accents (The Card Connection) • Vellum • Mini brads • Stamping ink • Embossing powder • Thread

The Number 7

Kimberly Kesti, Phoenix, Arizona

Kimberly celebrates the number 7 on this bold layout. The black and white combinations on the page add a dynamic look to the children's color photo mats. A house number makes a dramatic entrance into the reasons to love the number 7. The door beneath the domino opens to reveal Kimberly's hidden journaling.

supplies: Black, white, red, orange, yellow, green, light blue, purple and lavender papers • Printed transparency (Creative Imaginations) • Rub-on letters and bubble numbers (Li'l Davis) • House number • Ribbons (Offray and May Arts) • Hinges • Label maker (Dymo) • Domino • Georgia and Hootie fonts (Downloaded from the Internet)

a closer look

My Boys, My Loves

Shannon Zickel
Louisville, Kentucky

The smiles on the faces of Shannon's loves—her husband and son—light up this textural, heartfelt collage. Shannon created her own large journaling tag, covering it in canvas and adorning it with a fabric tie. She handwrote her journaling on the canvas, stamping the word "boys" to divide the two blocks.

supplies: Patterned papers (7 Gypsies, Me & My Big Ideas) • Foam letter stamps and paint (Making Memories) • Safety pins (Making Memories) • Buttons (Making Memories) • Stickers (Pebbles) • Letter stamps (PSX and Hero Arts) • Clay word accents (Li'l Davis) • Woven labels (Me & My Big Ideas) • Metal-rimmed circle tag (Avery) • Clips (7 Gypsies) • Brads (Creative Impressions) • Eyelet (Dritz) • Typewriter key (Creative Imaginations) • Label maker (Dymo) • Canvas • Fabric • Stamping inks

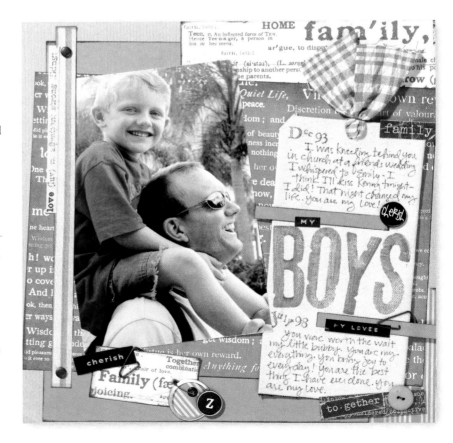

a closer look

Character

Laurel Gervitz, Maple Grove, Minnesota

With this page Laurel celebrated the many characteristics of the people in her life. Each black and white image lifts to reveal a color version accompanied by defining traits of each person. She embellished each portrait with words and accents relevant to each personality. The lower title block opens to journaling which summarizes the unique love Laurel has for her family.

supplies: Gray, black, red and ivory papers • Lace • Transparency • Ribbons • Elastic cording (7 Gypsies) • Metal spirals (7 Gypsies) • Metal binding loops (7 Gypsies) • Small eyelets (Making Memories) • Hinges (Making Memories) • Large eyelets (Magic Scraps) • Mini brads (Magic Scraps) • Clay phrase (Li'l Davis) • Brass button tacks (K & Co.) • Twill (Creative Impressions) • Paint • Red and black stamping inks • Computer fonts

open

closed

a closer look

Family

Suzy Plantamura, Laguna Niguel, California

A highly interactive family deserves a highly interactive page. Suzy designed this family gallery with six flip-ups that feature individual family members with detailed descriptions hidden beneath. The ties on the front open to reveal a page full of treasured family photos.

supplies: Patterned papers (Carolee's Creations, Creative Imaginations, K & Co., Anna Griffin, Daisy D's, 7 Gypsies) • Silk flowers • Ribbons • Lace (EK Success and Wrights) • Trim (Me & My Big Ideas) • Mesh (Magic Mesh) • Eyelets (Making Memories) • Brads (Making Memories) • Jump rings (Making Memories) • Metal and plastic letters, plastic words (K & Co.) • Word and letter stickers (Creative Imaginations) • Scrabble tiles • Rubber stamps (Hero Arts, EK Success, Ma Vinci's) • Raffia • Gold letter tags (Die Cuts With a View) • Mica • Stamping ink • (All following products: Li'l Davis) Safety pins • Wood frame • Epoxy words and letters • Frames

The Hudsons

Vanessa Hudson, Mt. Olive, Alabama

Shades of greens and tans lend a beachy feel to this page. Strips of corrugated paper with the corners wrapped in twine frame the focal photo. Dabs of modeling paste on the frame and background mimic white caps, while drops of extra thick embossing powder melted on the journaling block gives a water effect.

supplies: Blue paper • Patterned paper (Creative Imaginations) • Modeling paste (Liquitex) • Ultra thick embossing powder (Ranger) • Tiles • Stamps • Stamping ink • Fabric • Jute • Net • Birdhouse font (downloaded from the Internet) • (All following products: Making Memories) Brads • Washers • Charm • Sea shell plaque

August 2004

Laura Kurz, Gambrills, Maryland

Laura's layout reflects the simplicity of her family's favorite getaway. She used a corner rounder to lend a softer feel to the design. The swirling patterned papers flow with the beach theme, while large open space captures the feeling of peace and tranquility.

supplies: All papers (KI Memories) • Rub-on date (Autumn Leaves) • Letter rub-ons (KI Memories) • Word sticker (Creative Imaginations) • Renaissance font (twopeasinabucket.com)

Twins

Shannon Taylor (Masters '05)

Shannon's fascination with the relationship between twins peaked when she moved next-door to a pair. For her border, she cut away the white from patterned paper and then added clear gloss medium to the colored shapes. Shannon stamped, chalked and then added clear gloss to the title.

supplies: Patterned paper (SEI) • Lime and tan papers • Letter stamps (Fontwerks and Hero Arts) • Plastic letters (Colorbök) • Triangle jump rings (Making Memories) • Stamping ink • Chalks • Clear gloss (JudiKins) • Fabulous '50s font (scrapvillage.com)

The Same but Different

Shelley Rankin
Fredericton, New Brunswick, Canada

Shelley painted the underside of her printed title transparency and then highlighted words in the patterned paper. She smudged the paper, slide mounts, metal accents and envelope with paint.

supplies: Yellow and red papers (Bazzill) • Patterned paper (7 Gypsies) • Transparencies • Blue ribbon • Conchos (Scrapworks) • Label holders (Making Memories) • Letters and word phrase (Making Memories) • Slide mounts • Letter stamps (PSX) • Tag and envelope (Avery) • Metal screw • Paint

Together

Kathy Montgomery, Rocklin, California

Hidden journaling, tucked inside a stitched library-card pocket, tells of a mother's hope for her children's unending sibling love. Kathy gave her page a vintage look through a variety of distressing techniques. She created her own charms out of shrink plastic, using stamps and colored pencils to embellish them.

supplies: Light blue paper • Patterned papers (Paper Loft, SEI, Creative Imaginations) • Letter stamps (Stampers Anonymous, Stamps Happen, Inkadinkado, Renaissance, PSX and Ma Vinci's) • Epoxy word sticker (Creative Imaginations) • Ribbons • Shrink plastic • Colored pencils • Blending pen • Floss (DMC) • Metal photo corner (Making Memories) • Buttons • Copper brad • Acrylic paints • Stamping inks

Sibling Squeezing

Nic Howard (Masters '05)

Nic squeezed as many photos as she could onto her layout, using blocks of vellum to avoid a sense of overcrowding. The vellum softens the look and brings out the focal images on each page. Nic added rub-on letters over her handcut letters to illustrate the expressions of love between her children.

supplies: Light blue and gray papers • Vellum • (All following products: Making Memories) Ribbon • Definition stickers • Circle tags • Rub-on letters • Foam letter stamps • Paint • Silver brads • Silver eyelets • Black stamping ink • LB Bonus Marci font (downloaded from the Internet)

Brotherly Love

Sharon Laakkonen, Savannah, Georgia

When Sharon's daughter, Brittany Laakkonen, took this photo of her three brothers, Sharon knew it would be perfect for a scrapbook page. She loved the way this photo captured how these three rely and lean on each other... even if they don't always get along.

supplies: White, sage and avocado green papers • Patterned papers (KI Memories) • Transparency • Computer fonts

Simply Sherrie

Pamela James, Ventura, California

Pamela employed a computerized machine embroidery program to create the borders for this tribute to her sister, Sherrie. The black-and-white childhood photos lead up to a current, color image on top of the journaling book. Pamela transformed monogrammed letters into medallions, which she used to begin each title word.

supplies: Sage, pink and lavender papers (Bazzill) • Ribbon (Offray) • Pearls (Westrim) • Embroidery thread (DMC) • Label holders (Making Memories) • Lace • White felt • Brads • White acrylic paint • Varnish • Machine embroidery program • Computer fonts

Brothers

Shannon Brown, St. Helens, Oregon

Bright colors provide the perfect background for Shannon's black-and-white photos. She found this design to be a great way to document the boys' closeness and relationship development over the course of her younger son's first year. She used paint to create the border frame on the left, and then brushed it on the backs of her vellum journaling blocks.

supplies: Blue paper • Patterned paper and die cuts (KI Memories) • Vellum • (All following products: Making Memories) Letter stamps • Photo anchor • Brad • Word charm • Acrylic paint • Computer font

10 Things

Kimberly Kett
St. Catharines, Ontario, Canada

Kimberly had her two daughters list 10 things they like about each other and printed the lists for this page. She kept the design simple, with torn edges, a folded corner and flower accents providing dimension. Small lengths of ribbon lend delicate shine.

supplies: Sage, cream and pink papers (Bazzill) • Patterned papers (Daisy D's) • Number stickers (EK Success) • Flower punch • Foam letter stamps (Making Memories) • Stamping ink (Stampin' Up) • Flowers • Ribbon • Eyelets • Computer font

A Mother's Heart

Angelia Wigginton
Belmont, Mississippi

Angelia used soft colors and feminine frills and bows on this layout celebrating motherhood. This page, dedicated to her second daughter, shares a mother's thoughts, hopes and dreams for their relationship together. Rickrack, stitching and buttons lend the softness to this page.

supplies: Lime, peach and cream papers • Patterned paper (K & Co.) • Silk ribbon • Buttons (Junkitz) • Heart charm • Vellum • Rickrack • Silver leafing pen • Mistral font (downloaded from the Internet) • Chestnuts font (twopeasinabucket.com)

Always

Angelia Wigginton, Belmont, Mississippi

Angelia's soft and sentimental layout expresses her unending love for her daughters in dreamy patterns. The bows on the right of the page are tied to tags that reveal further black-and-white images of each daughter. By raising the focal photo with foam adhesive and adding decorative corners, Angelia establishes the illusion of peering through a window.

supplies: Patterned papers (Daisy D's) • Vellum (The Paper Co.) • Eyelets (Making Memories) • Metal corners and metal clock charm (K & Co.) • Gingham ribbon (SEI) • Mini brads • Foam adhesive • Stamping ink • Computer fonts

a closer look

Bananas, Too!

Brandi Barnes, Kelso, Tennessee

The "Why?" stage of toddlers is represented in the journaled conversation Brandi had with her daughter at the mall. She enlarged one of the photo-booth images, converted it into black-and-white, and printed it on textured paper for her focal photo. By tilting the photo strip and scattering the photo turns, she captures the chaotic frustration of this classic event.

supplies: Vanilla and textured white papers (Chatterbox and Bazzill) • Patterned papers (KI Memories and Chatterbox) • Snaps (Making Memories) • Brads (Making Memories) • Photo turns (Making Memories) • Label maker (Dymo) • Computer fonts

U Stole My Heart

Donna Pittard, Kingwood, Texas

This birthday page has a special place in Donna's heart, as it not only features her favorite photo of her twins, but a favorite time of life. The photo was taken just before they both regressed into autism, and the hinged card opens to tell the emotional tale. Extra thick embossing enamel covers many page elements and gives them a shiny finish.

supplies: Chip, thistle and flesh-tone papers • Patterned papers (7 Gypsies and K & Co.) • Cream vellum (National Cardstock) • Cheesecloth • Die-cut letters and door pull (Foofala) • Metal letters and hinges (Making Memories) • Antique brass brads (American Tag) • Jewelry tag (American Tag) • Aged tag (7 Gypsies) • Mosaic stamp (Stampers Anonymous) • Bubble resin numbers (K & Co.) • Fibers (Flights of Fancy) • Photo corners • Ultra thick embossing enamel (Ranger) • VersaMark watermark ink (Tsukineko) • Sepia ink • Dark brown thread • Computer fonts

Don't Go Far

Carrie O'Donnell
Newbury, Massachusetts

Carrie went for complete innovation when creating this two-page, vertical layout. She created the illusion of an extra large photo by cutting the image in half using image-editing software and then printing each half on 8½ x 11" sheets of paper. The patterned slide mount frames and wooden words capture the character of a little red wagon, while a metal label holder posing as a license plate on the focal photo lends playful charm to a touching moment.

supplies: Brick red paper • Patterned papers (The Paper Loft) • Title letters and stencil (Autumn Leaves) • Patterned slide mounts (Li'l Davis) • Wooden words (AbsolutelyEverything.com) • Label holder (EK Success) • Muslin • Sandpaper • Twine • Red stamping ink • Georgia font (Microsoft)

Don't go far. As I stand behind the lens, watching as my 3 boys head down the block, all I can think of is how I don't want this moment to end. I love watching the 3 of you together, enjoying each other's company & all that surrounds you. I can't believe how fast you are growing up. Hopefully you will enjoy every moment along the way. I'll let the 3 of you go...off to explore...just you boys. Please don't grow up too fast...and don't go too far.

My Greatest Love

Robyn Lantz
Charlestown, New Hampshire

Robyn discovered that the road less traveled often leads to loves unimaginable. To record this lesson she stamped "My Boys" onto patterned paper, and then overlaid a printed transparency, which she embellished with letter accents to complete the title. The focal photo crowns a fabric-covered, posterboard card, which opens to journaling about Robyn's gratitude and appreciation for her family.

supplies: Black and cream papers • Patterned papers (All My Memories, K & Co.) • Heart tag and transparency (Creative Imaginations) • Clasp (7 Gypsies) • Label maker (Dymo) • Bottle cap letters (Li'l Davis) • Letter stamps (PSX) • Nostalgiques paper clip (EK Success) • Fiber • Black floss (DMC) • Fabric (Dan River) • Posterboard • Stazon black solvent ink (Tsukineko) • (All following product: Making Memories) Foam letter stamps • Paint • Brads • Photo corners • Metal tiles • Heart paper clip • Ribbon • Label holder • Safety pin

Cut From the Same Cloth

Tamara Morrison
Trabuco Canyon, California

Tamara's two favorite guys are at their best on this layout that describes the father and son's many similarities. The photo highlights the visual distinctions between her husband and "Mini Matt," while the journaling unveils the little things that are shared in their special bond. Torn fabric swatches and a zipper illustrate the title phrase.

supplies: Navy and white-speckled papers • Fiber (Timeless Touches) • Label maker (Dymo) • Die-cut letters (Quickutz) • Rub-on letters (Scrapworks) • Safety pin (Li'l Davis) • Tom's New Roman font (downloaded from the Internet) • (All following products: Junkitz) Fabric • Zipper • Jump ring • Woven label • Button

Reece and Matt are alike in so many ways. The physical resemblance between them is uncanny, right down to the same cowlick in their hair, but the similarities don't end there. They have the same goofy sense of humor, the same talent for making sound effects, and the same short temper. Both are early risers, nature lovers, and attention hogs. They even both sleep with one foot sticking out of the covers. No wonder Reece has earned the nickname, "Mini Matt"!

Whether working together in the yard, watching old movies, or just going to the grocery store (where they make sure to visit the walk-in refrigerator and do a silly dance inside – one of their many private jokes), the special bond my two favorite guys share is always evident. They have a deep understanding of one another that will hopefully last all their lives. They are made from the same mold, two peas in a pod, cut from the same cloth.

Photo: February, 2003

Journaling: July, 2004

PHOTO: BELL PHOTOGRAPHY (LARGE PHOTO)

Ethan

Lorinda King, Rigby, Idaho

This layout documents the life of Lorinda's son from baby to young man. A large, current photo graces the left-hand page and guards the pocketed note from Mom. The right page displays the metamorphosis from tot to teen in a timeline accented by expressive labels. A printed twill band binds the two pages.

supplies: Black paper • Patterned papers (Paper Loft, Carolee's) • Label maker (Dymo) • Printed twill tape and silver clasp (7 Gypsies) • Altered file folder (Rusty Pickle) • Large square punch (Marvy) • Twine • Black stamping ink • (All following products: Carolee's) Cloth letters • Weathered tag • Frame • (All following product: Making Memories) Metal letter • Rub-on letters • Date stamp

I Love You

Amy Warren, Tyler, Texas

Colorful snapshots are framed in negative strips on the side of Amy's page. The bright papers running across the background give a joyful vibrancy and movement to the page.

supplies: Dark and light purple, orange and red papers • Handmade paper • Transparency frame • Negatives strips (Creative imaginations) • Ribbons • Printed ribbon (Making Memories) • Metal words (Making Memories) • Metal words (All My Memories) • Charm • Buttons • Paint • Computer fonts

The 2 Faces of Two

Michelle Pendleton, Colorado Springs, Colorado

This design captures the many moods of a 2-year-old. Michelle created this page to show the sweet, affectionate side of her son first. Lift the photo to find journaling and photos, showing the underworld of being 2. Michelle distressed the papers with smudges and smears true to toddler form.

supplies: Cream, light, medium and dark blue papers • Patterned papers (NRN, K & Co., Carolee's) • Fibers (On the Surface, Scrapworks) • Letter conchos (Colorbök) • Wooden letter (Walnut Hollow) • Rubber stamp (Stampendous) • Canvas number (Li'l Davis) • Tacks (Chatterbox) • Twill tape • Small brads • Jump ring • Chalk • Stamping inks • Chalk inks • Safety pins • Mod Podge (Plaid) • Aleene's Paper Glaze (Duncan) • Computer fonts • (All following products: Making Memories) Foam stamps • Rub-ons • Tags • Floss

a closer look

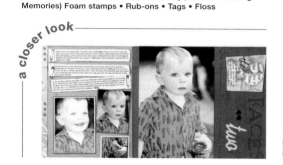

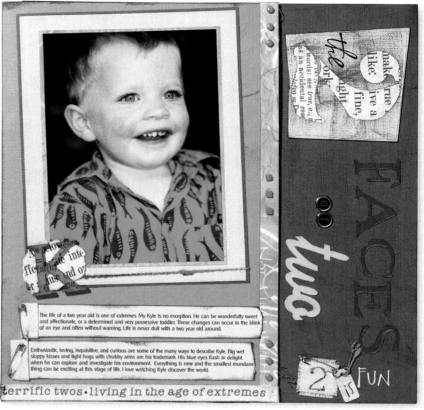

The life of a two year old is one of extremes. My Kyle is no exception. He can be wonderfully sweet and affectionate, or a determined and very possessive toddler. These changes can occur in the blink of an eye and often without warning. Life is never dull with a two year old around.

Enthusiastic, loving, inquisitive, and curious are some of the many ways to describe Kyle. Big wet sloppy kisses and tight hugs with chubby arms are his trademark. His blue eyes flash in delight when he can explore and investigate his environment. Everything is new and the smallest mundane thing can be exciting at this stage of life. I love watching Kyle discover the world.

terrific twos • living in the age of extremes

It All Adds Up

Jenn Brookover (Masters '05)

Jenn's layout was inspired by a conversation she had with a friend one day, as they began doing the math on being a mom. Being the mother of four boys makes for some pretty astounding numbers! She created the photo mat for the main photo using artist scratchboard, which is fairly light, acid-free and easy to scratch with the provided tool. She placed her stencil directly on the board and scratched away the desired effect. The printed twill runs the theme across the page, while horizontal and vertically placed statistics provide movement and visual energy.

supplies: Brown, tan and cream papers • Patterned papers (Carolee's, Sweetwater) • Twill tape (7 Gypsies) • Black ribbon (Making Memories) • Buttons (Blumenthal Lansing) • Scratchboard (Ampersand Art Supply) • Metal number (Making Memories) • Acrylic paint (Making Memories) • Letter stencils • Floss (DMC) • Chalk • Taupe and black stamping inks • Computer fonts

My Girl

Shelley Rankin
Fredericton, New Brunswick, Canada

Shelley was so fond of the sweet shabby chic style she saw on a layout by Michelle Minken, marketing manager, in a previous *Memory Makers* issue, that she put her inspiration to work with this photo of her and her daughter. The stitched fabric border coordinates with the frayed fabric photo mat and snap accents and evokes a feeling of comfort. A collage of strung flowers, buttons, fabric pieces and twist-tie words is kept confined by striped page borders and an underlying striped design.

supplies: Patterned papers (Anna Griffin, Sweetwater, Making Memories and K & Co.) • Striped fabric swatches, labels and buttons (Junkitz) • Silk flowers • Letter stickers (Wordsworth) • Elastic (7 Gypsies) • Letter stamps (Hero Arts) • Copper phrases (K & Co.) • Snaps • Staples • Paint • Stamping ink• (All following products: Making Memories) Ribbon • Safety pins • Label holders

Forever

Vanessa Hudson, Mount Olive, Alabama

To create the look of a well-loved quilt, Vanessa wet, crumpled, sanded and inked her patterned papers, and then machine-stitched them for the pieced-fabric appearance. She hand tinted a photo and printed a reproduction on matte paper, which lends a tranquil, timeless effect. Unhook the elastic band and lift the journaling block to explore further photos, which peek through the vellum journaling.

supplies: Red and light blue papers (Bazzill) • Patterned papers (Daisy D's) • Photo corners (Canson) • Ribbon (Li'l Davis) • Clasp (JHB International) • Vellum • Button • Fabric • Elastic • Rickrack • Stamping ink • Computer font • (All following products: Making Memories) Hinges • Safety pins • Brads

a closer look

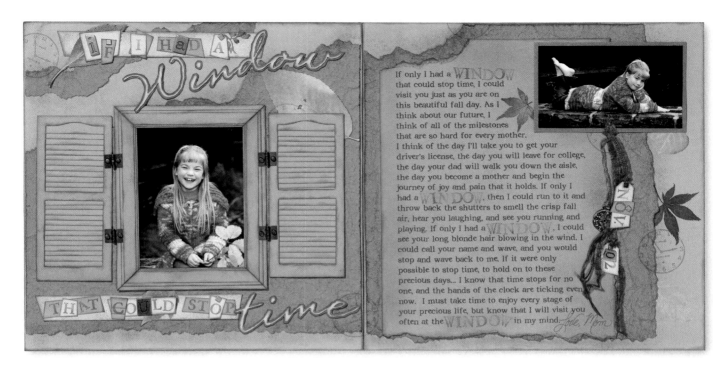

If I Had a Window

Vanessa Hudson, Mount Olive, Alabama

Vanessa created her own window of time to preserve the image of her daughter at a treasured stage in life. She transferred the beautiful autumn day onto her layout, using rich colors, embellishments and textures that warm the senses. She designed the shutters herself by layering strips of paper, inking in between for a shadowy effect. The hinges lend realism and dimension, and pull the page together with the metal letter accents.

supplies: Olive, tan, cream and orange papers (Bazzill) • Leaves (Nature's Pressed) • Fibers (EK Success) • Clock charm (7 Gypsies) • Clock stamp (Inkadinkado) • Letter and number stamps (Hero Arts) • Stamping ink • Computer font • (All following products: Making Memories) Metal letters • Brads • Hinges

My Greatest Love

Jlyne Hanback, Biloxi, Mississippi

This inviting layout was the result of Jlyne's desire to highlight extensive journaling and many photos of her daughter in one design. She succeeded by stitching pockets into printed vellum and filling each with a tag that captures a portion of her daughter's sweet personality. The stitching, lace and flowers bring a feminine quality to the page, while the vertical strips bring out Domonique's spunky personality.

supplies: Burgundy and scarlet papers (Chatterbox) • Ivory lace • Silk flowers • Watson font (Chatterbox font CD) • (All Following products: Chatterbox) Patterned papers • Vellum • Die-cut Love tiles • Shaped tacks

Job Description

Julie Johnson (Masters '05)

The job descriptions related to being a mom or a dad are filled by Julie and her husband on this humorous, interactive layout. Julie's page contains a folder, which when opened shows her job application tucked inside and lists her son's firsts on the timesheet below. The same is continued inside her husband Darryl's paperwork, with the list of firsts growing longer. Julie chose bright and tender moments for her photos to demonstrate what the best jobs look like.

supplies: Brown paper (Chatterbox) • File folders (Autumn Leaves) • Label maker (Dymo) • Letter stencils • Job applications • Stamps • Round letter tags (Making Memories • Ribbons (Making Memories) • Fabric (Printed Treasures by Milliken) • Library cards (Limited Edition) • Clock charm (7 Gypsies) • Short Cuts brush-on paint (Krylon)

Grimm Family

Alecia Grimm, Atlanta, Georgia

Inspired by her mother's annual Christmas newsletter, Alecia found it rewarding to create an album including each "year in review." This page highlights her ever-changing, ever-growing family. She painted and chalked her molding to blend with the page and add just a hint of formality. The letter "G" stencil sparks the theme words for the page, all beginning with the first letter from their family name.

supplies: Cream paper • Moulding (Making Memories) • Patterned papers (7 Gypsies and Daisy D's, Paper Loft) • Definition stickers (Karen Foster) • Letter stencil • Label maker (Dymo) • Letter brad (Jo-Ann) • Brads (Karen Foster) • Mesh • Staples • Paint • Chalk • Computer font

Complete

Nic Howard (Masters '05)

Soft colors against stark black and white give a modern flair to this milestone moment in Nic's family. Nic created her own patterned paper by printing a dictionary definition onto vellum. She handcut her title, stamped it in graduating tones with watermark ink, and then clear embossed. Tiny glass marbles at the corner of the embossed, vellum journaling block add decorative texture and softness to this tender moment.

supplies: Black, white, light green and pink papers • Vellum (Stamp It) • Safety pins (Making Memories) • Tag templates • Letter stickers (SEI) • Lettering template (Wordsworth) • Tiny glass marbles • Thread • Beads • Versamark watermark stamping ink (Tsukineko) • Clear embossing powder • Hot Chocolate font (twopeasinabucket.com)

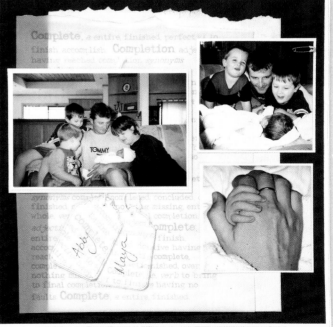

open

closed

Love Notes

Saralyn Berkowitz, Long Beach, New York

Unzip the zipper and flip up the title (shown left), and confessions of love with photos as evidence are revealed on this page. The bottom half of the page is a pocket, holding reproductions of love letters collected from Saralyn and her husband's courtship. Small photos are collaged with scraps of love note patterned papers. Wooden tiles spell "love" while rub-on letters on tags spell out "notes."

supplies: Patterned paper (7 Gypsies, Carolee's, Pebbles, K & Co.) • Wooden letters (Li'l Davis) • Rub-on letters (Li'l Davis) • Zipper (Junkitz) • Label maker (Dymo) • Transparency • Brads (Making Memories) • Tags (Making Memories) • Harting and Scriptina fonts (downloaded from the Internet)

Our Love Story

Pamela Rawn, Champlin, Minnesota

Pamela created a mini book of photos and journaling that documents the love story of the Rawn family. The book opens to the right, adding a unique quality to her layout. She cut the book cover from a transparency sheet and stamped her title directly onto it with acrylic paint. Festive fibers bring a wind-blown whimsy to the page, perfect for a Harley-ride effect.

supplies: Red, black and cream papers (Bazzill) • Printed transparency and stickers (Creative Imaginations) • Bottle caps (Li'l Davis) • (All following products: Making Memories) rub-ons, decorative brad, ribbon, and photo corner • Letter stamps (EK Success) • Word charm • Fibers • Buttons • Stamping ink • Michele font (downloaded from the Internet)

You and Me

Samantha Walker (Masters '05)

Where the focal photo left off, Samantha continued the scenery by painting an oceanscape onto the next page of this spread. She cut the painting into strips, inked the edges and stitched it to navy paper. She printed her title onto blue paper, drew over the letters with a watermark pen and then heat set it with white embossing powder. Mini shadow boxes line the bottom of the page, created of frames painted with gesso and watercolors. The shells and sandpaper swatches are reminiscent of the beach.

supplies: Brown and blue papers • Watercolor paper • Watercolor paint (Windsor Newton) • Gesso (Grumbacher) • Mesh paper (FLAX) • Tags (Stampin' Up) • Brown stamping ink (Stampin' Up) • Metal frames and quote plaque (Making Memories) • Raffia • Thread • Shells • Pearls • Clock • Sandpaper • Black rapidiograph pen • Versamark watermark pen (Tsukineko) • White embossing powder

a closer look

Top 10 List Album

Play with this unique album format to create a humorous yet moving tribute album.

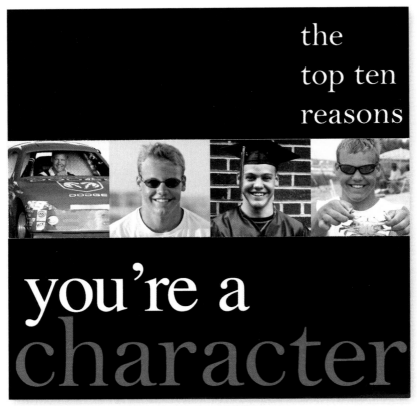

the top ten reasons

you're a character

supplies: Black paper (Bazzill) • Patterned paper (Rusty Pickle and MOD) • Rub-on words (Rusty Pickle) • Rub-on numbers (Autumn Leaves) • InDesign and Photoshop image-editing software (Adobe) • 8 x 8" postbound album (Westrim) • Computer fonts

Highlight the outstanding characteristics of a sibling, spouse or parent with a Top 10 list album. For inspiration, recall David Letterman's popular top 10 list. You can include as many reasons as you desire. Start with your photos to inspire your list.

Joanna Bolick (Masters '04) created this 8 x 8" album for her 19-year-old brother, Mark, using the Top 10 format to list the reasons he is a character. Though the format is light-hearted and fun, the overall message is heartfelt and moving.

Joanna suggests including a dedication page that explains why you're creating the album for the person; you can place it after the title page. To make the computer-generated title page shown left, Joanna created a photo bar with image-editing software, using four photos from her selection of 10.

As you turn the album's title page, the album begins with reason number 10 and counts backwards. We begin the countdown below and include Joanna's album tips.

Keep it simple and uniform

"I recommend keeping the album simple," says Joanna. "It's easier when creating multiple pages to stick to a uniform design." Joanna sized each photo and created her text with image-editing software. For cohesiveness, Joanna adhered a strip of black paper on one side and a strip of patterned paper on the top or bottom of each page. "I chose patterned paper that would match the photos after I printed out each one," says Joanna. On this page, she plays up her brother's sporty, daring side.

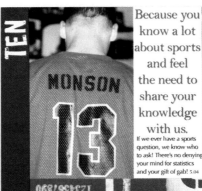

Because you know a lot about sports and feel the need to share your knowledge with us.

If we ever have a sports question, we know who to ask! There's no denying your mind for statistics and your gift of gab! 5.04

Because you're dangerous behind the wheel.

Okay, okay, so Dad says that you're supposedly a good driver. But we have to tease you a little, don't we? After all, you're a race car fan, and you seem to feel the need to speed! 7.04

Get others involved

"The Top 10 list is written from my sister Kristina's and my perspectives as Mark's older (and loving) sisters," say Joanna. On this page, the loving sisters celebrate the fashionable and personable characteristics of their brother.

Because you look good in any outfit.

From baseball outfits (remember that fourth of July costume?) to tuxes, you know how to pull off the look! Although we may not admit this to you, you do clean up well! We're proud of the many "hats" you've worn in life, from a responsible high school student and employee to a fun-loving, committed college student. 6.00

Because you can talk to anybody about anything.

You even managed to talk your way into a first class plane ticket! As stated before, you have the gift of gab. You also have that unique ability to discuss a variety of topics while making a person feel completely at ease. 7.04

Because your future is bright.

You're a high school graduate! How does it feel? We're proud of your high school accomplishments and the desire you have to succeed now that you're in college. We hope the future brings many successes and provides fulfilment for whatever career path you choose. 5.04

Because there's always a hint of mischief behind that grin.

Just because you're wearing shades doesn't mean that we can't tell that you're up to something! You're quite the prankster, despite your disarming grin and air of innocence. We honestly don't know how you've fooled everyone for so long now! 7.04

Include the date

"I know that in the future there's no way I'll be able to easily remember which year such-and-such happened, " says Joanna. That's why on each page, she included the date the photo was taken. Here she recalls a proud moment—Mark's high school graduation—then lightens the spread by teasing him about his mischievous grin.

Be lighthearted

"Mark has endured a lot growing up in a household with two big sisters, so we tried to poke fun at that aspect," says Joanna about reasons four and three. After taking credit for his survival skills, big sister pokes fun at Mark's fish tales.

Because you've learned the art of survival growing up with two older sisters.

We might have picked on you just a bit when we were growing up, but what else are sisters for? Just remember, we love you! 7.04

Because the fish is always bigger in your version of the story.

Sure, we believe you. Just like the time you caught that large-mouth bass on Grandma's lake, right? You've been known to tell a tall tale or two...7.04

Because you're a thoughtful uncle, brother, and son.

You show your concern for each member of our family through your humor, your emails, and your gifts. Thank you for that! 5.04

Because you'll always be our "little" brother.

Since you've gone from being the smallest in the family to the tallest, we now have to look up to you! Although we're well aware of the irony in that fact, we don't want you to forget that you will always be our baby brother. So just remember, if we're ever in a car together again on a long road trip, you're still stuck in the middle seat. Between us, your sisters who love you. 10.86

Show appreciation

Despite their poking fun, the two sisters end the album on a heartwarming note, showing appreciation for their "little" brother.

Through the Years

Celebrate life's seasons of change in your scrapbook.

by Heather A. Eades

To every page we turn, turn, turn in our albums, there should be seasons of memories shared with those whose roots run deep in our hearts. And while fashion, hairstyles and outward circumstances may change, the love between our family and friends endures.

Our times to weep and laugh, mourn and dance, celebrate births and pay tribute to lives lived are meant to be shared. So as you look through these timeless page ideas from our Masters that celebrate life through the years, be inspired to make your own pages about relationships that run deep even through seasons of change.

Like Not a Day Has Passed

No matter the miles apart or time past, some friendships pick up right where they left off, as Jodi L. Heinen illustrates here on this page about her friendship with the other Jodi L. Heinen. The two friends are not related—it is merely a coincidence that they both married men with the same last name! Jodi changed the photos to sepia to remedy the poor quality of older photos. This established a warm color scheme. A red silk daisy hints at her friend's vibrant personality while adding a burst of color.

supplies: Red and cream papers • Patterned paper (Daisy D's) • Buttons (Making Memories) • Ribbon (Making Memories) • Silk flower • Bottle cap • Thread • Stamping ink

like not a day has passed

Understand that friends come and go, but with a precious few you should hold on. Work hard to bridge the gaps in geography and lifestyle, because the older you get, the more you need the people who knew you when you were young.

- Mary Schmich

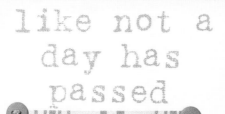

cherish

togetherness

Jodi & Jodi

I remember those initial snotty words she uttered to me that first week of junior high - "So, how many pairs of Gloria Vanderbilt jeans do you own?" With those words so began our friendship.

Our friendship grew despite all of our differences. She was into make-up. I liked make-up but couldn't pull it off. She lived in the country and I lived in town. I was in sports. She was a cheerleader. She was a beauty queen and I was average. Through those trying years of junior/senior high we shared secrets, had fun, got in trouble and established a life-long friendship. After high school, we truly took different paths. I went to college and lived a single girl's life - going out, dating and moving a couple times a year. Jodi went to work, married her high school sweetheart, started a family and bought a house.

The one true constant in our relationship is the level of comfort we have with each other. We can go for a few years without talking and our next conversation occurs without missing a beat. We never small talk, we dive right into conversation as though we spoke with each other just the day before. After 24 years there is this unspoken familiarity that allows us to continue on our own separate journeys through life and yet our friendship remains like not a day has passed.

A Terrific Nine Years

To a couple in love, time stands still, though photographs will tell you otherwise. Samantha Walker designed this colorful memory timeline to keep tabs on those milestone moments of her and her husband's nine years together. Using vibrant colors for her photo tags, she attached a black-and-white image and a woven phrase accent word for each year. She then brushed white paint to highlight the journaling and to unify the spread. Colorful staples, festive paper clips and sentiment labels accent the couple's story.

supplies: Black, red, green, blue, purple and yellow papers • White acrylic paint (Plaid) • Black and brown stamping inks • Classic shadow die-cut letters and Threads woven labels (Me & My Big Ideas) • Paper clips • (All following products: Making Memories) Paper labels • Staples • Metal letter • Brads

Home

Jessie Baldwin designed this page to reflect on the homes she and her family lived in during her childhood. She stamped her title onto door patterned paper and expanded the theme by creating coordinating door-shaped photo mats and journaling blocks. In her journaling, Jessie evoked memories from each abode, appealing to all five senses. Metal-rimmed vellum tags specify the dates of inhabitance for each location.

supplies: Deep purple, yellow, red, olive and peach papers • Patterned paper (Mustard Moon) • Tags and brads (Making Memories) • Ribbons (Anna Griffin) • Letter stamps (Ma Vinci's) • Stamping ink • Pen • Charms

1976–1978

1978–1979

1980–1989

1989–1995

I see... "The Old House"
on O'Bannon Drive
I smell... the pungent
eucalyptus trees
I feel... piano keys
I taste... mac & cheese
with hot dogs for
dinner
I hear... lions roaring
at 4pm for dinner

I see... Puerto Rico
I smell... the salty air
of the Caribbean
I feel... the soft
Flokati rug in
the living room
I taste... coconuts from
Cagui's backyard
I hear... the song of
the coqui

I see... Concord Green,
Massachusetts
I smell... family dinner
cooking at the
Tripodi's house
I feel... the worms on
the sidewalk
after the rain
I taste... a bunny cake
for my birthday
I hear... the "Grease"
soundtrack on
Dad's record
player

I see... the house my
parents still
live in
I smell... my mom's
perfume
I feel... the cool tile
floor underfoot
I taste... Thanksgiving
dinner every year
I hear... Les Miserables
on the CD player

Brother

A time-spanning collage of brotherly love celebrates the bond between Sheila Doherty's husband and his bro. A combination of black-and-white and color photos creates a dynamic energy on the page, balanced by the inked journaling block on the left. Sheila had her husband write about his indescribable relationship with his brother, using actual quotes and memories from their childhood and beyond.

supplies: Dark and light blue papers • Love patterned paper (Outdoors & More) • Definition patterned paper (7 Gypsies) • Make It Suede textured paint (Krylon) • Letter stencil (Headline Signs) • Alphabet stamps (Hero Arts and PSX) • Definition travel labels (Pebbles) • Stickers (Karen Foster) • I Kandee twist ties (Pebbles) • Lowercase canvas and bubble letters (Li'l Davis) • Watch-face stick pin (EK Success) • Threads woven labels (Me & My Big Ideas) • Watch face die cut (Maya Road) • Embroidery thread • Textured Trios ribbons (Michaels) • Photo corners (Canson) • Photo anchors • Mini brads • Eyelet word and rub-on letters (Making Memories) • Acrylic paint • Distress Ink Antique linen and Walnut stamping ink (Ranger) • Black stamping ink

Then and Now

Recording the timeless joy and laughter between her parents served a double benefit for Nic Howard. Not only did she now have visuals of her parents' "careful" and carefree relationship on one page—she got to hear stories as her mom aided in the photo-selection process. Nic played up the humor between her parents' odd-couple marriage through the journaling, but established a classic, timeless tone through her color scheme.

supplies: Olive, beige and cream papers • Patterned paper (Basicgrey) • Pixie alphabet stamps (PSX) • Walnut Distress Ink (Ranger) • Icicles acrylic letters (KI Memories) • Ribbons • Flower accent • White paint

Looking back through the years it's easy to see that humour has always played an integral part of Mum and Dad's lives. From this engagement photo when Mum was only 18 years old, to the most recent photos of them together, the strength of the relationship is obvious.

People have always laughed at my Mum and Dad. My Dad is the most highly-strung guy I know, and Mum is the easy going carefree lady. It was neat to dig up an old engagement photo of theirs and ask Mum all about it. Mum was only 18 and she says Dad was the same way back then. The stress Dad has to have to get through each day was always there, as was the easy going attitude my Mum adopted to avoid the stresses.

Be Careful, Be CAREFUL! For goodness sake, BE CAREFUL! Dad is the guy most likely to be screaming this across the room, as you are doing something not really scary at all. We have always laughed at Dad's ability to worry over anything. We all enjoy the banter Mum and Dad share with their very different personalities. It'll be Dad pacing beside the BBQ waiting for the meat to cook to perfection, and it'll be Dad pacing beside your car as you back out the driveway to make sure you get it just right. Mum will be as relaxed and happy as ever, just watching the show.
They say opposites attract.

I collected some photos from through the years that show their relationship. From the laughs they have had on holiday, to dressing up as Santa at Christmas time, to the good old happy family times we have had.

through the years

then

and now

Bob & Mary Jane

With years of heartwarming photos to choose from, deciding which images of her grandparents to use on this tribute proved to be Jenn Brookover's biggest challenge. She narrowed it down to one photo per decade and used image-editing software to unify size and brightness. Vintage-patterned fabric paper complements the era of the 1944 focal photo.

supplies: Olive green and red embossed papers • Patterned papers (Paper Love and Flair) • Fabric paper (Michael Miller) • Coins (Boxer) • Wooden letters (Li'l Davis) • Label maker (Dymo) • Flowers (Jo-Ann) • Rub-on letters (Chatterbox) • Transparency • Brads • (All following products: Making Memories) Ribbons • Mailbox letters • Staples

Cousins

The friendships found in family are celebrated here on Jeniece Higgins' layout, showcasing the nostalgic fabrics she has shared with her cousin. She designed her page with the theme of clothes across time, and filed her journaling in mini folders beside each photo. Actual fabric swatches and button accents clothe this page in style.

supplies: Patterned papers (Me & My Big Ideas, Autumn Leaves, Daisy D's) • Flower and rub-on letters (Making Memories) • File folders and tiny tags (DMD) • Letter stamps (PSX and Hero Arts) • Canvas envelope and wooden letters (Li'l Davis) • Rub-on letters (Provo Craft) • Brads • Stazon solvent ink (Tsukineko) • Paint and Instant Age Varnish (Delta) • Corduroy • Buttons • Trim

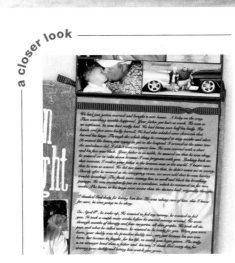

A Reason to Fight

True-blue heroism defines Julie Johnson's husband on this page, applauding him for his courageous efforts to recover from an accident to be there for his son. The focal photo flips up to reveal emotion-laden journaling printed on vellum, overlaying an 8 x 10" photo. Julie also included a photo collage of father-and-son moments underneath the flip cover, celebrating the silly, the serious and the sentimental.

supplies: Weathered paper (Paper Loft) • Dark blue paper • Ribbon (Making Memories and Li'l Davis) • Metal word (Colorbök) • Brads • Alphabet stamps (Making Memories and River City Rubber) • Déjà Views rub-ons (C-Thru) • Transparency • Vellum • Paint

WE'RE HALF-IDENTICAL!

I know, you're scratching your head thinking there's no such thing as half-identical. But it's true! All during our growing up years, Cindy and I wondered whether we were really identical or not. There were things about us
so incredibly unique (i.e. same birthmarks and distinct eyes) that it seemed we must be identical, but then how could we have such different teeth? It just didn't add up.

Then one day in 1987 Cindy called me with some incredible news... we are half-identical! The latest issue of Time Magazine had a special article on twins and revealed that there are more kinds of twins than just identical and fraternal. In the case of half-identical twins, (are you ready for the biology lesson?) an egg that is splitting is fertilized by two different sperms, resulting in twins that share the same genetic material from the mother but unique genetic material from the father. And that explains our differences exactly! For the most part both of us take after Mom, but Cindy has a bit more of Mom in her facial structure and I have a bit more of Dad in my facial structure.

So the mystery has finally been solved! We are a very rare (I imagine) and unique kind of twins, we're HALF-IDENTICAL!!!

Identical Twins

A compilation of comparisons and contrasts over time between twin sisters makes up this two-page treasure by Christine Brown. A chronological band of side-by-side shots on the left are complemented by pull-out tags, showcasing the duo's differences and similarities. A hidden journaling feature behind the "best friends" photo (shown left) answers the title question. The twins are half-identical—a true, but rare biological possibility.

supplies: Patterned paper (Daisy D's) • Transparency (Hammermill) • Label tab (Autumn Leaves) • Embroidery floss (DMC) • Micron pen (Sakura) • (All following products: Making Memories) Flowers • Definitions • Buttons • Metal words • Brads • Acrylic paint • Foam stamps

A LIFE LIVED

I can't say that I remember ever being a "daddy's girl" as a child. Mom said I was a bit when I was very young. I wish I remembered those times more. I do remember his desire to teach me practical things & it drove me crazy, like taking me shopping for a vise grip & making me call auto shops for parts. It completely stressed me out. I guess I just didn't understand him. But things changed in 1994 when Dad moved to Arizona for a job. Somehow, the distance made our father/daughter bond stronger. We talked by phone frequently. He called when he needed advice about dating. I called him with good new about the boys and scrapbooking (he introduced me to photography). I felt very close to him. It was a wonderful feeling knowing he was always there. Unfortunately, in 2003 he was diagnosed with Leukemia & given only 2 short months to live. I was devastated! I was able to spend a week with him before he passed away. He told me stories of his life. I made sure to write them down and I've included his life story in the book below.

2003

1970

Dad

LARGE
50% Teacher
40% Hero
10% Friend

Cool iron
Manmade materials

a closer look

A Life Lived

An accordion card stitched into fabric provided the perfect mini album for Shannon Taylor to extensively document her father's life. She filled the small book with numerous photos, papers and embellishments that celebrate the course of his life. She dangled a charming childhood photo from the cover of the album to contrast with the image from his later years in life.

supplies: Black, lime and orange papers • Coral textured paper • Plastic letters (Colorbök) • Label maker (Dymo) • Accordion card (Rusty Pickle) • Circle frame (Pebbles) • Acrylic paint (Making Memories) • Oval green tag (Making Memories) • Ribbon • Thread • Brads • Transparency • (All following products: Junkitz) Fabric • Fabric buttons • "Dad" label • Zipper

Extended Family

Gallery

Pages for the people far and near
who enrich our lives.

Father-in-law

Grandmother

Uncle

Cousin

Mother-in-law

Grandfather

Aunt

Cousin

Father-in-law

AleX & PopPop

Love

Perfect Love

Wendy Inman
Virginia Beach, Virginia

Wendy let the simplicity of
perfect love between her son
and his great-grandfather guide
the design of this page. She
stamped the flower in metallic
copper that adds a joyful glow,
while strips of patterned paper
and a blue sticker border play up
the linear elements of the photo.
A couple of words constructed
with letter stickers in the title
highlight key words while meld-
ing with the page as a whole.

supplies: Yellow-orange paper (Bazzill)
• Patterned paper (SEI) • Stickers (SEI) •
Letter stamps (PSX) • Colorbox copper
stamping ink (Clearsnap) • Rub-on (Making
Memories) • Flower foam stamp • Paint •
Metallic rub-ons (Craf-T)

Blessed Be

Tenika Morrison, Puyallup, Washington

Seeing her 1-year-old son walk hand-in-hand down the beach with his 78-year-old great-grandfather was priceless to Tenika, who designed this computer-generated page to savor the moment. She used a sun design to blend the boundaries between the two photos and rich blues to reflect the beauty of the ocean.

supplies: Photoshop 7.0 image-editing software (Adobe)

Simple Pleasures With Pappy

Jackie Siperko, Dallas, Pennsylvania

The simple pleasure of sharing Popsicles with their great-grandfather are the memories Jackie wants her boys to cherish. She kept this page basic and down-to-earth, reflecting those uncluttered moments. A leather frame around the date, along with leather corner accents, works with the brown paint wisps to commemorate this extraordinarily ordinary day.

supplies: Patterned paper (Carolee's Creations) • Beige paper (Bazzill) • Brads • Leather strips • Scriptina font (downloaded from the Internet) • (All following products: Making Memories) Leather frame • Rub-on letters and numbers • Paint

Abuelo, Nieto

Doris Sander, Hermitage, Tennessee

Doris created this page to treasure her son's
first visit to meet his grandparents (abuelos)
in Honduras. His grandpa wrote the poem that
is nestled beside his photo. Foreign coins, a
charm and sheer strips lend themselves to the
setting of this trip.

supplies: Tan, brown, orange and olive papers (Bazzill) •
Patterned papers (7 Gypsies, K & Co.) • Ribbon • Frame, epoxy
letters, and wax thread (7 Gypsies) • Eyelets (Making Memories)
• Brads (Making Memories) • Rub-ons (Making Memories)
• Letter stamps and stamping ink (Stampin' Up) • Tag • Cardboard
frame • Vellum • Coins • Computer font • (All following products:
Li'l Davis) Label holder • Word plate • Charm • Epoxy letter "g"

A Girl and Her Poppa

Traci Turchin, Hampton, Virginia

Designing this page in memory of her grandpa
allowed Traci to preserve their relationship. The
colors for the page were inspired from the pajama
print in the photo. She stamped flowers with
watermark ink at the bottom of the page, leaving
an imprint, much like her grandpa made on her.

supplies: Blue, light and dark pink papers (Bazzill) • Ribbon •
Flower stamp (Impress) • Versamark watermark ink (Tsukineko) •
Plain Jane font (downloaded from the Internet)

Riding with Papa Dick

Pam Weisenburger
Seeley Lake, Montana

Pam grabbed her camera when she saw her son and father coming down the road. She created this rugged-boy layout by adhering the focal photo and buttons to the page with wire. She brushed acrylic paint over sanded photo edges, twill tape, the title and journaling. She printed digitally altered versions of the photo in index format and cut them into filmstrips, and then buttoned them in place along with the journaling strip.

supplies: Patterned paper (Karen Foster) • Blue papers (Bazzill) • Black paper (Paper Garden) • Twill tape (Wrights) • Wire • Buttons • Acrylic paint (Delta) • Channel Tuning and Batik Regular fonts (downloaded from the Internet)

Will You Love Them?

Shelley Rankin, Fredericton,
New Brunswick, Canada

For Shelley, this page serves as a visual response to a conversation with her dad many years prior. At 18, her insecurities at their peak, she asked her adoptive father if, when she had children some day, he would love them as much as his other grandchildren. The photo on this page nods an unquestionable reply, and she journaled the details of this healing moment. Dark colors collaged with distressed metal and paper accents define this loving, grandfatherly design.

supplies: Black paper (Bazzill) • Patterned papers (7 Gypsies, Paper Loft, Anna Griffin) • Charms twist ties (Pebbles) • Stencil (Autumn Leaves) • Stickers (Wordsworth) • Letter stickers (Chatterbox) • Label holder (Li'l Davis) • Metal-rimmed tag (Deluxe Designs) • Canvas • (All following products: Making Memories) Moulding strips • Woven labels • Decorative brads • Page pebbles • Photo turns

Remember

Breanne Crawford, Scotch Plains, New Jersey

The Irish smile of Breanne's grandfather pops from this page made in remembrance of his legacy of love. The unique swirl accent she created from rub-on words on paper strips affixed by square brads gives a playful measure to the layout. Breanne's journaling shares her heartfelt stories and sentiments behind the man whose image illuminates this tribute.

supplies: Patterned paper (Provo Craft) • Tan paper • Vellum • Computer font • (All following products: Making Memories) Printed ribbon • Label holder • Brads • Rub-ons

He's That Kind of Grandpa

Tarri Botwinski, Grand Rapids, Michigan

Tarri designed this spread as a tribute to a special grandpa. Layers of warm, friendly patterned papers capture the feel of the photos, while jovial printed ribbons are buckled in place. Tarri journaled a list of all the qualities that define her father-in-law as a grandpa. Geometric-shaped tacks continue the theme of play while serving as bullets for each special "grandpa-ism."

supplies: Patterned papers (7 Gypsies and Chatterbox) • Brown and olive papers (Bazzill) • Printed ribbon, buckle and eyelets (Making Memories) • Rub-ons and shaped tacks (Chatterbox) • Fibers (Fibers by the Yard) • Stamping inks (Clearsnap and Close to My Heart) • Pens (Marvy) • CAC Crazy Legs and CAC Leslie fonts (downloaded from the Internet) • OhGoody font (Chatterbox)

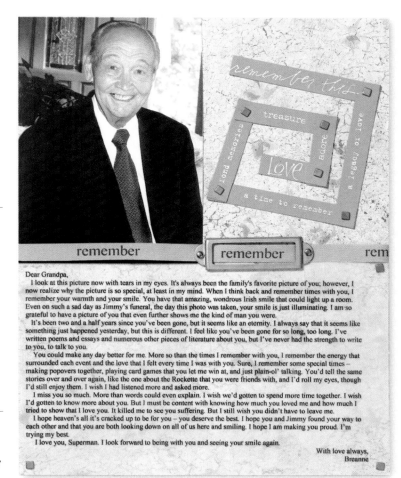

Dear Grandpa,
I look at this picture now with tears in my eyes. It's always been the family's favorite picture of you; however, I now realize why the picture is so special, at least in my mind. When I think back and remember times with you, I remember your warmth and your smile. You have that amazing, wondrous Irish smile that could light up a room. Even on such a sad day as Jimmy's funeral, the day this photo was taken, your smile is just illuminating. I am so grateful to have a picture of you that even further shows me the kind of man you were.

It's been two and a half years since you've been gone, but it seems like an eternity. I always say that it seems like something just happened yesterday, but this is different. I feel like you've been gone for so long, too long. I've written poems and essays and numerous other pieces of literature about you, but I've never had the strength to write to you, to talk to you.

You could make any day better for me. More so than the times I remember with you, I remember the energy that surrounded each event and the love that I felt every time I was with you. Sure, I remember some special times – making popovers together, playing card games that you let me win at, and just plain-ol' talking. You'd tell the same stories over and over again, like the one about the Rockette that you were friends with, and I'd roll my eyes, though I'd still enjoy them. I wish I had listened more and asked more.

I miss you so much. More than words could even explain. I wish we'd gotten to spend more time together. I wish I'd gotten to know more about you. But I must be content with knowing how much you loved me and how much I tried to show that I love you. It killed me to see you suffering. But I still wish you didn't have to leave me.

I hope heaven's all it's cracked up to be for you – you deserve the best. I hope you and Jimmy found your way to each other and that you are both looking down on all of us here and smiling. I hope I am making you proud. I'm trying my best.

I love you, Superman. I look forward to being with you and seeing your smile again.

With love always,
Breanne

Not Just Cousins, But Friends

Shelly Umbanhowar, Phoenix, Arizona

Aaron and his cousin Ethan are the stars of this page. Shelly layered patterned papers and added brightly colored ribbons and rickrack for a collaged feel, bursting with the energy of two young boys. She hinged the lower photo, which opens to reveal journaling adhered to the back. Mini tags fastened by brads lend a playful element to the title.

supplies: Dark blue paper (Bazzill) • Patterned papers (KI Memories) • Letter stamps (Rusty Pickle) • Rub-on letters (Scrapworks) • Label maker (Dymo) • Green and blue sheer ribbons (Li'l Davis) • Rickrack • Brads (All My Memories) • Tab (Autumn Leaves) • Black stamping ink (Ranger) • Computer font • (All following products: Making Memories) Date stamp • Hinges • Mini tags

It's All About the Cousins

Deb Perry
Newport News, Virginia

For her title, Deb placed a transparency over the large photo and stamped around the images, following the flow of the pose itself. She used rub-ons for the smaller words, wrapping them around the arrangement. Brads used as flower centers add dimension. These four cousins have always had a blast playing together, and Deb journals their fun-filled festivities at Auntie's house in extensive detail.

supplies: Brown paper (Bazzill) • Patterned papers (KI Memories and American Crafts) • Decorative brads (Karen Foster) • Vellum pink flower (artist's own design) • Number sticker (K & Co.) • Black fine pen (Creative Memories) • Papyrus font (dafont.com) • (All following products: Making Memories) Rub-on letters • Foam letter stamps • Pink acrylic paint

Cuteness...It's a Family Trait

Misty Posey, Decatur, Alabama

Misty arranged her page celebration of these two cousins to emphasize their effervescent personalities. By angling buttons in spontaneous arrangements, and angling letter stickers in opposing directions, she captures the fun, energy and sweetness in one perky design. Aqua stamping ink and vibrant pink buttons play happily against the pastel color scheme and express the joy of this family friendship.

supplies: Light blue, pink and gray papers (Club Scrap and Bazzill) • Patterned paper (KI Memories) • Letter stickers (Club Scrap) • Foam stamps (Making Memories • Buttons (Making Memories) • Metallic accent (Die Cuts with a View) • Brads (Bazzill) • Versamagic turquoise stamping ink pad (Tsukineko) • Buttons • Flowerchild and Olive Oil fonts (downloaded from the Internet)

Second Cousins

Julie Johnson (Masters '05)

Julie's layout celebrates the unique closeness between the fourth generation living not only in the same state but in the same city! She used neutral tones for the page, with only the title providing bold definition in red. She wrote each child's name on tabs adhered to the right side of the photo, listing them down the line. Tokens, buttons and multimedia letters carry the sepia tones of the photo throughout the page, while drawing out similar tones from the patterned paper.

supplies: Black papers (Bazzill) • Patterned paper (Paper Loft) • Paper tabs (7 Gypsies) • Sticker (Sweetwater) • Embellished paper clip (EK Success) • Ribbons (EK Success and Making Memories) • Buckle (Karen Foster) • Brads (Making Memories) • Metal letters (Making Memories and Li'l Davis) • Flowers • Token • Chipboard letters (Li'l Davis) • Transparency

A Cousin Is a...Friend

Tina Powell, Sutherland, Virginia

Tina celebrates the friendship of cousins on this spread. One color photo makes a dynamic impact on the sepia-tone collage of patterned and solid papers. The crackle patterned paper and ink-edged sepia photo lend a vintage feel to the layout.

supplies: Orange and cream papers • Patterned papers • Letter tags • Label holder • Vellum quote (Tiny Tales) • Word stickers (Bo-Bunny) • Typewriter key stickers (EK Success) • Slide mount • Raffia • Ribbon • Brown stamping ink • (All following products: Making Memories) Snaps • Alphabet stamp • Definitions • Clips

Together Is the Best Place...

Amy L. Barrett-Arthur, Liberty Township, Ohio

Amy designed this page to celebrate the closeness of these cousins. To coordinate both masculine and feminine elements on the page, Amy used leather flowers and screw-top snaps and a balance of bright colors with smudges of inks and paint.

supplies: Navy and red papers (Bazzill) • Patterned papers (Daisy D's and Li'l Davis) • Letter stencil • Letter stickers (Creative Imaginations) • Label maker (Dymo) • Tag (7 Gypsies) • Fabric (Jo-Ann) • Letter stamps (Hero Arts) • Black and brown stamping inks • (All following products: Making Memories) Flowers • Brads • Screw snaps • Foam letter stamps • Paint

Rub-a-Dub Dub

Sherry Laffoon, Modesto, California

After a day of playing on their Aunt's farm, these three cousins cooled off in the horse trough. Sherry used refreshingly cool colors to offset the warmth of the sepia-toned prints. She stitched pockets into the strip at the top of the page and dunked her title tags inside. Layering patterned paper behind the number stencil at the bottom provided the perfect accent to coordinate with the gingham ribbons that add country charm.

supplies: Black paper (DMD) • Patterned papers (EK Success, Karen Foster, Bo-Bunny, Paper Adventures) • Ribbons (May Arts and Offray) • Thread (Coats and Clark) • Rub-on letters (Making Memories) • Stencil • Stickers (Once Upon A Scribble and Li'l Davis) • Brads • Eyelets • Felix Titling font (downloaded from the Internet)

Cousins Are Flowers

Melissa Boyd, Douglasville, Georgia

Melissa celebrates the closeness of second cousins on this spread. The tab on the focal photo lifts to reveal journaling about the special friendships. Stitched fringe adds texture and a border to the title block. The illusion of a hanging photo is created with looped ribbon and eyelet snaps. Melissa applied an image-editing software filter to the gray photo for an embossed effect.

supplies: Patterned paper (Chatterbox) • Antique alphabet stamps (PSX) • Stamping ink • Eyelet snaps (Making Memories) • Ribbon (7 Gypsies) • Photo corners (Scrapgoods) • Fringe • Photoshop image-editing software (Adobe) • 2Peas Dream font (twopeasinabucket.com) • Floralies font (downloaded from the Internet)

Your Andersen Uncles

Shannon Brown, St. Helens, Oregon

Shannon bridged the distance between her son and his many uncles, ranging in age from 13-22, by creating this layout to celebrate their love. At a Christmas visit, Shannon captured the fond moments shared by the boys on film. She kept the design simple and masculine, with black-and-white photos on sage and tan paper. Jute, punch labels and screw-shaped eyelets lend boyish fun to the page.

supplies: Sage, tan and dark brown papers • Patterned papers (Flair) • Eyelets and date stamp (Making Memories) • Letter stickers (Wordsworth) • Label maker (Dymo) • Jute • Slick Writer pen (American Crafts)

Uncle Terry

Tara Pollard Pakosta, Libertyville, Illinois

Tara's big brother is the favorite uncle to her daughter, and she designed this layout to embrace their unique bond. From rides on four-wheelers to berry and apple picking, these two enjoy time together. Muted colors and distressed papers create a masculine feel while the black-and-white photo adds a soft touch.

supplies: Sage and blue paper (Making Memories) • Patterned papers (Chatterbox) • Stencil letter • Photo turn (7 Gypsies) • Word sticker (Sweetwater) • Ribbon (Li'l Davis) • Letter stamps (PSX) • Colorbox Fluid Chalk brown ink (Clearsnap) • (All following products: Making Memories) • Foam stamp • Acrylic paint • Brad

Simple Bond

Tina Barriscale, Nepean, Ontario, Canada

Tina designed this page about the bond between her son and her sister. She created a background by layering patterned paper hearts over white paper and then placing a printed transparency on top. She mounted her photos on white paper, leaving room for a journaling transparency as well. Red accents tie in the photos.

supplies: White paper (KI Memories) • Patterned paper (7 Gypsies) • Printed transparency (Creative Imaginations) • Clips (7 Gypsies) • Ribbon (Making Memories) • Word tiles (KI Memories) • Rub-on letters (Me & My Big Ideas) • Negative strip (Creative Imaginations) • Transparency • Apple Garamond font (downloaded from the Internet)

Aunt Christy

Melissa Smith, North Richland Hills, Texas

Melissa lovingly dedicates this layout to her sister's advice to her nieces—Melissa's daughters. A stamped scroll pattern accents the photos. Melissa kept the layout simple with advice clips, photos and a few ribbon and charm accents.

supplies: Patterned paper (Rusty Pickle, Basicgrey, Anna Griffin) • Letter stickers (Anna Griffin) • Stamp (Hobby Lobby) • Transparency • Beads • Ribbon • Ribbon charms • Baskerville Oldface font (downloaded from the Internet)

Mutual Adoration

Jenn Brookover (Masters '05)

Jenn created this page to record the bond between her son and his grandma. For her titled photo mat, she printed the title and then cut around the letters. She rubbed chalk onto the back of the cutout letters, taped it in place on scratchboard and then traced over the letters to transfer the chalk. Applying varying pressure with a scratching tool, Jenn outlined the letters.

supplies: Patterned papers • Label holders, ribbon and snaps (Making Memories) • Charms (Card Collection) • Scratchboard (Ampersand Art) • Button • Stamping ink • Acrylic paint • CAC One Seventy, Amaze and Typist fonts (downloaded from the Internet)

A New Tradition

Angie Head (Masters '04)

Two new traditions were established for Angie's family after this cookie-making event: Christmas in Arkansas and baking cookies! Angie wrote out the cookie recipe on a card and hinged it to reveal her journaling underneath. Soft green tones and crimson accents let the bright faces of the photos make this layout a sweet success.

supplies: Green, red and natural papers • Patterned paper • Letter stamps (Wordsworth and Making Memories) • Date stamp • Recipe card • Buttons • Stamping ink (Stampin' Up) • (All following products: Making Memories) Hinges • Label holder • Definition sticker • Printed ribbon

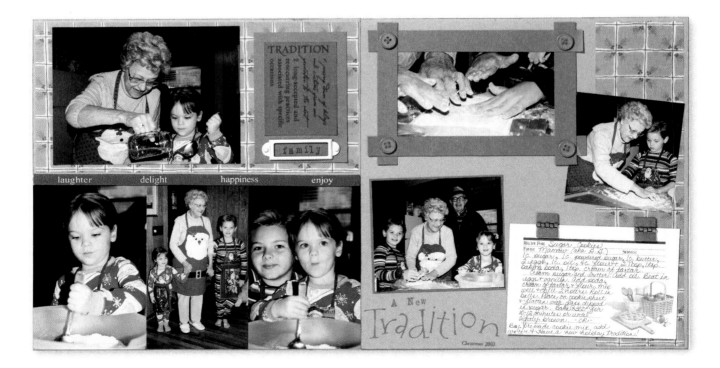

Our Nana Rocks

Ginger McSwain, Cary, North Carolina

Ginger captured these images of all five grandchildren having a blast with their Nana. She enlarged the focal photo to zoom in on the happy faces. Her bright colors and merry patterns radiate an exhilarating energy, perfect for defining this day. Ginger accented the layout with game stubs held fast with brightly colored snaps.

supplies: Patterned paper (SEI) • Yellow paper • Snaps (Making Memories) • Game tickets • Vinyl Stickons font (flyerstarter.com) • Vulgar Display of Power fonts (1001fonts.com) • Computer font

From Granddaughter to Grandmother

Debby Shelton, Painesville, Ohio

Becoming a grandma took Debby back in time to moments with her own grandmother. She added a mix of patterned papers to tie in the focal photo. The flowers add a joyful quality to the page.

supplies: Red, black and yellow papers • Patterned papers (7 Gypsies) • Daisy die cuts (Paperhouse) • Sticky Pics sunflower and white daisy stickers (Paperhouse) • Sonnets letter sticker (Creative Imaginations) • Typewriter key and mini brush letter stickers (EK Success) • Stamping inks • Dotlets eyelets (Doodlebug) • Eyelets • Ribbon • Tag • Floss (DMC) • Paper yarn • Dom Casual D font (downloaded from the Internet) • (All following products: Making Memories) Definition sticker • Ribbon charm • Yellow snaps

Great-Grandmother

Angie Head (Masters '04)

The sweet embrace shared between great-grandmother and child are tenderly swaddled here on Angie's layout with lace and pearls. Angie adhered lace directly onto her photos to hide the empty space, rather than cropping. She threaded ribbon through netting and attached it to the right side of the page for a textural border. She customized her premade tag with a gold leafing pen and added the word "great" for a finishing touch.

supplies: Patterned paper • Olive paper (Anna Griffin and National Cardstock) • Letter sticker (EK Success) • Leafing pens (Krylon) • Tag (EK Success) • Paper ribbon • Lace • Trim • Ribbon • Netting • Buttons

Kissy Monster

Miki Benedict
Modesto, California

Fabric swatches combined with gingham ribbon and country-charm buttons make a visit from Great-Grandma's "Kissy Monster" leap off the page. Miki was able to keep a boyish look about the page, using a soft, yet masculine, color scheme. The patterns and textures lend warmth. Miki tucked descriptive words for each small photo inside the buttonhole sticker-strip along the bottom of the page.

supplies: Patterned papers (Sweetwater) • Tan paper (Bazzill) • Fabric swatches (Junkitz) • Button-hole sticker strip (Sweetwater) • Word stickers (Sweetwater) • Fabric buttons and clothing tag (Junkitz) • Heart buttons (Doodlebug) • Ribbon • Letter stickers (Pebbles and EK Success) • Fibers • Garth Hand font (downloaded from the Internet)

Agga and Ryan

Diana Hudson (Masters '04)

Life lessons and love, linking the past to the future, are shared between Diana's son and his grandmother, as she documents on this page. To achieve the look of a quilt without all the work of paper piecing, she machine stitched along the squares of her patterned paper. Diana also traced and cut an oval from a transparency to cover the oval vellum tag, adhering the monograms before attaching the transparency. The rich patterns and colors, tassels and trim all work together with the metal accents and faux wax seals for a masculine, noble flair.

supplies: Patterned papers (EK Success and Basicgrey) • Blue trim • Faux wax seals • Tag • Monogram stickers and tassels (EK Success) • Paige letter die (Quickutz) • Architexture embellishments (EK Success) • Paper clips (EK Success) • Transparencies • Fancy Free font (twopeasinabucket.com)

Beautiful Grandchildren

Danielle Thompson, Tucker, Georgia

For Danielle, designing a layout with all the coziness of her grandparents' home was the goal. She created a vintage look, "like an old, worn, familiar quilt," by printing vignetted photos and emotive journaling onto transparencies. She then placed the transparencies over highly textured papers and old lace trim. She used image-editing software to turn her photos black-and-white and faded the edges for an aged look. She created her own title letters with clay, rubber stamps and flower stickers.

supplies: Patterned paper (Chatterbox and Anna Griffin) • Embossed paper (Lasting Impressions) • Transparencies • Metal photo corners and charms (Embellish It) • Lace trim (Hobby Lobby) • Beads • Pewter accent corners (Hobby Lobby) • Medallion (K & Co.) • Nailheads (Jewelcraft) • Silk flowers • Vintage greeting card • Clay • Letter stamps • Flower embellishment stickers (Blumenthal Lansing) • Floss • Rub-ons (Making Memories) • Ribbon (Offray) • Keepsake pocket (Pebbles) • Fibers (On the Surface) • Silver frame (Nunn) • Pin embellishment (EK Success) • Eyelets (Doodlebug) • Stamping ink • Dimensional paint and acrylic paint (Delta) • Chalks (Craf-T) • Piano Recital font (twopeasinabucket.com)

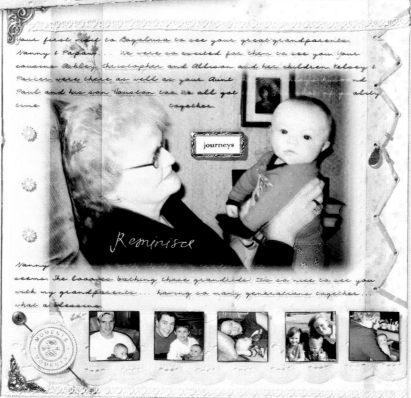

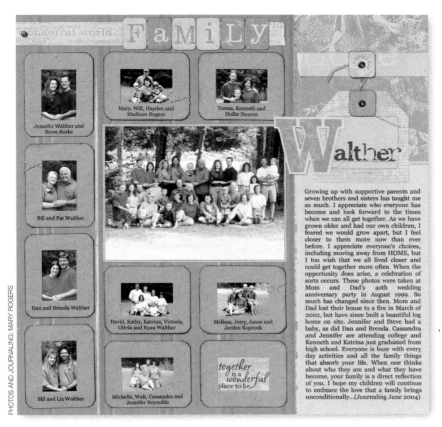

PHOTOS AND JOURNALING: MARY ROGERS

Walther Family

Diana Hudson (Masters '03)

Mary Rogers of Au Train, Michigan, comes from a large family shown left. Showcasing the individuals as well as unifying the entire brood on a page can be a daunting task. Inspired by Mary's idea to frame individual families in slide-mount windows, Diana designed this page with Mary's photos. Diana adhere the slide mounts to a sheet of paper and then ran it through a printer, identifying the many faces interwoven in the larger family photo. Each immediate family member wore the same colored shirt, which works as a great identifier in the large extended family portrait. Diana incorporated Mary's words into the design on a printed journaling block.

supplies: Patterned papers (C-Thru and Rusty Pickle) • Slide mounts (DMD) • Tag, letter and square die cuts (C-Thru) • Eyelets and brads (Making Memories) • Letter rub-ons (Autumn Leaves) • Linen thread (Hillcreek) • Stamping ink • Computer font

Embrace Moments Like This

Suzy West, Fremont, California

Hugs and laughter, smiles and strength—these are the elements to embrace in a close and loving family such as Suzy's. She designed this page to capture the excitement and energy of their family gatherings. The tied ribbons at the bottom of the page provide eye-pleasing textures and illustrate the bond that knits this group together. The large, painted title stretches across the page yet is linked with the separate title strips.

supplies: Blue, brown and avocado papers • Patterned papers (KI Memories) • Daisy • Ribbons • Eyelets • Transparency • Photo corners • Paint • Stamping ink

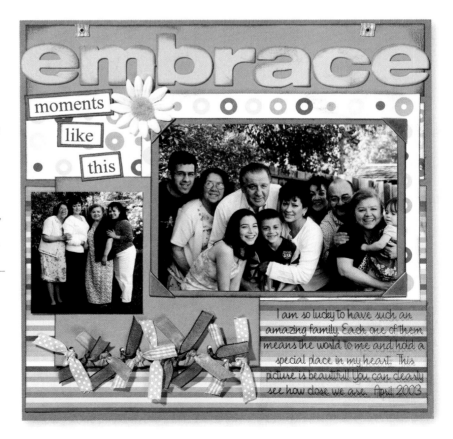

Tribute Letters Album

Honor a loved one with an album filled with letters and memories he or she will treasure for a lifetime.

Honor an extraordinary person or couple in your life or commemorate a milestone with a tribute-letter album. Ask family, friends or colleagues to pay tribute by writing a letter of appreciation. Showcase all of the letters along with photos of the authors in a sentimental album.

After collecting handwritten letters and photos from all 13 grandchildren, Denise Tucker (Masters '04) created an elegant 8 x 8" tribute album for her parents—Grandpa and Grandma Thompson. The album begins with a title page, a dedication page, a timeline that lists the all the grandchildren and their birthdates and then the table of contents.

For the title page shown left, Denise showcased a portrait taken on her parents' 50th wedding anniversary. Floral tapestry patterned paper adds a classic look while brown stamping ink adds a vintage flair. Denise painted embossed metal strips and title letters and then dabbed them with purple ink. Vintage buttons threaded with embroidery floss and sheer ribbon add a timeless touch.

album supplies: Beige and burgundy papers • Patterned paper (Rusty Pickle) • Vellum • Album (K & Co.) • Embossed metal strips (Making Memories) • Embossed letter tiles (EK Success) • Envelope closures (EK Success) • Embossing powder • Paint (Plaid) • Ribbon (Stampendous) • Distress Ink (Ranger) • Purple stamping ink (Stamp Craft) • Vintage buttons • Floss • Computer font

Denise had her nieces and nephews fold a sheet of white paper in half and write why they appreciate their grandparents or a special memory. "Even the baby drew scribbles," says Denise. She scanned the letters, printed them on beige paper then inked the edges. She inserted each letter into a standard envelope, which she labeled and distressed with ink.

Jessica

"Your relationship has been a great example during a time in our society when families are often deteriorating."

Elizabeth

"In your reassuring routines I sensed a larger feeling of peace and order in this world."

By using common elements such as threaded buttons and copper brads throughout, Denise unified the album. All of the grandchildren's names appear under acrylic label holders on beige paper distressed with ink. Denise found different ways to secure the letters on each page. On Jessica's page above left, Denise made an envelope out of the patterned paper then added a folio closure. On Elizabeth's page above right, she created a custom pocket by cutting the patterned paper into a triangle then folding the edges under. On Tanner's page below left, the letter is tucked under embossed metal strips attached with brads. On the page featuring three grandchildren below right, she made a large pocket decorated with ribbon and painted rivets. Denise printed a quote pulled from each child's letter onto vellum and then heat embossed.

quick tip

Put a time limit on returning letters and send frequent reminders. Then find creative ways to include the letters on the pages.

I remember one Christmas when you gave me one of my favorite X-box games. I now continue to think of you each time I play it.

Tanner

from: *Tanner*

Elysse   *Emylee*   *Clayten*

Music Soothes the Soul

D

A man, a guitar, and a few chords... To his young children he is a rock star, to his older children he has immense talent, and to me he is the music in my life.

2004

When creating heartfelt pages about those you love, be deliberate with every decision. Michelle Pendleton composed these photos, wrote this journaling and designed this page with one thing in mind—capturing the role music plays in her husband's life. Read through the following pages for tips to create layouts that exude emotion and personality.

supplies: Green, blue, slate, tan, cream, black and brown papers • Music patterned paper • Photoshop image-editing software (Adobe) • Fibers • Cork • Metal-rimmed tags (Making Memories) • Brads • Circle punch • Corner rounder • Phoebe letter dies (Quickutz) • Alphabet stamps • Embroidery floss • Vintage Photo stamping ink (Ranger) • Stazon black solvent ink (Tsukineko) • Black dye ink • Number stamps • Freebooter Script, Typewriter Oldstyle, Eras Light, Tag Script and Monogram fonts (downloaded from the Internet)

Heart & Soul

A 3-step guide to crafting pages that capture the character of your loved ones

Look at the scrapbook page shown on the left. Chances are, you do not personally know the subject, let alone recognize him. Stop and take an extended look—study the photographs, absorb the journaling and take note of how the page design complements the photos and journaling. Based on this scrapbook page, do you now feel as if you gain insight about this man's personality?

Three ingredients melded together to create this revealing page: interpretive photos, heartfelt journaling and mood-enhancing page design. These ingredients are necessary to create scrapbook pages that capture character. This article breaks down the process of creating such scrapbook pages.

We asked scrapbook artist Michelle Pendleton of Colorado Springs, Colorado, to create three scrapbook pages about one important person in her life—her husband, Dwayne. Her challenge: Each page had to celebrate a core aspect of Dwayne's character, and each page had to be independent in mood and spirit from the others. The result: three pages that show rich character development.

step 1

take interpretive photos   **62**

step 2

write heartfelt journaling   **66**

step 3

design with emotion   **70**

step 1 | Take Interpretive Photos

Photos are the cornerstone of any scrapbook page. When creating a page that digs to the root of a loved one, a scrapbooker must begin with interpretive photos. Interpretive photos allow viewers to relate to the subject. They are filled with emotion and proof of a personality. Use the following tips to take your own interpretive photos.

by Kelli Noto (Masters '03)

Wen creating a scrapbook page about a loved one, the photos should capture the spirit of the subject. To capture this spirit, your photos need to interpret, not document, the subject to convey his or her personality.

A documentary photo shows a moment in time, but an interpretive photo goes beyond the moment and speaks to the memories that we would like to keep. Interpretive photos tell more than just the who, what, where and when—they reach into the why and how.

Go beyond snapshots with this step-by-step guide to interpretive photographs that will reveal the personalities and relationships of those whom you love.

documentation versus interpretation

A driver's license photo documents its subject. It looks like the person, but it is notorious for being unflattering. The pose is in-your-face; the flash is harsh. Shown below is Dwayne Pendleton's driver's license photo. It looks like him, but a viewer cannot learn anything about who Dwayne is by looking at it.

An interpretive photo has an entirely different feel. Next to Dwayne's driver's license photo is a photo that his wife, Michelle, took for the layout on page 84. Dwayne appears to be in his element—he is outside at a favorite park, cradling his beloved guitar in his arms; he looks relaxed and happy. This picture captures him and something important to him—the relationship he has with music.

Interpretive photos can enhance scrapbook pages and make them more engaging. They tell a story about the important people in your life, what it is about them that you love, the relationships that are important to you and your core values. Interpretive photographs can help to capture the feelings and thoughts that make up the reasons why you scrapbook.

an interpretive photo dissected

location:
outdoor, comfortable and familiar location

time of day:
mid-morning, when Dwayne is cheeriest

clothing:
neutral, plain shirt and denim that complements, not distracts

personality:
subject is posed with meaningful item, a guitar

plan for a photo shoot

Most interpretive photos don't just happen; they require planning. There are three things to think about when planning a photo shoot: finding a suitable location with great natural light; timing—think about the time of day when your subject is happiest; and clothing. You can direct your subject on what to wear, or let his or her wardrobe make a personal statement. Count on shooting an entire roll of film to catch a variety of expressions and to get that one particular shot that will melt your heart.

Location is pivotal in the final outcome of your portrait. Choose a place that is simple enough to keep the focus on your subject. Try to find a familiar place to make your subject feel more comfortable, but avoid any high-traffic areas. Parks can be wonderful photo locations as can your backyard or porch. Look for a spot that benefits from natural light—natural light will complement your subject.

If photographing outdoors, stick to the shade or take pictures when the sun is low in the sky to avoid squinting and harsh shadows. If your front porch has wonderful natural light and a simple background such as a brick wall, then it's the perfect spot.

Or, try the garage. Look at the light just inside the garage—what

The documentary photo on Dwayne Pendleton's driver's license is utilitarian—it simply shows what he looks like. The photo on the right, taken by his wife Michelle, offers a window into who Dwayne is.

would happen if you hung a sheet or piece of fabric over the clutter and used the open garage door as a natural light source? A garage is a great place for a home photo studio.

You can take photos inside, but beware of the flash. A camera flash can wash out people and leave a deer-in-the-headlights feel to a picture. Have your subject sit next to a large window or use a higher speed film to avoid the harshness of the flash. In the photo on page 89, Michelle Pendleton used the light from a large window to light her husband's and sons' faces. You can use a fill flash or reflect the light with a white sheet or piece of foam core if shadows exist on one side.

Perhaps the best secret to great interpretive photos is a happy subject. Be sure your subject is rested, comfortable and fed. For example, if you are photographing a young child, plan your session around the time of day that he or she tends to be in lively spirits. Make the session fun by singing songs or playing games. Conversely, if photographing an adult, 6 p.m. on a summer weekday evening before dinner may not be the best bet. The light may be wonderful, but your subject's attitude may not be if his or her mind is still reeling from the stresses of the day, and he or she is hungry for supper.

Simple clothes work best for photos of this nature. Soft pastels and denims will highlight the face. Avoid busy patterns, stripes and writing; they detract from the person's face.

use posing and light

The next step in taking interpretive photos is customizing your session to your subject. If you want his or her personality to show, put your subject in comfortable surroundings doing things he or she loves.

Think about it this way: If your loved one were to have an article published about him or her in *Time* magazine, what kinds of photos would the article include? What kinds of expressions would he or she be wearing? What would the background look like? Would he or she be engaged in a favorite activity? If so, what?

In regard to capturing personality, an easy place to start is with basic posing. On the most basic level, use posing to enhance gender characteristics. When posing a man, angle the camera slightly below him and square his shoulders to the camera (see photos above). Photographing him at an upward angle will emphasize his broad shoulders, making him look more masculine.

When posing a woman, use a higher camera position and angle her shoulders to the right or left of the lens for a more slimming and feminine feel.

Basic posing guidelines and a lower, straight-on camera angle contributed to these successful photos. Michelle Pendleton had her husband pose in a natural setting with a treasured item that he could also lean on, which helped him relax.

To ease your subject, allow him or her to lean against something. Also, try giving the person something to hold. In the photos above, Michelle asked her husband to dress in his cycling attire and posed him with his bike. His body is relaxed against the bike, and he looks more natural. If you're working with small children, don't feel like you have to pose them. Great candids can happen when you just let them play while you snap away.

Next, determine the type of lighting you will want. Lighting helps determine the attitude of your interpretive portrait. On-camera flash suggests a snapshot, while soft light conveys romance, innocence and warmth. Soft lighting is available in the shade or on a cloudy day. It tends to flatter women by minimizing wrinkles and other skin imperfections.

Directional light, like that coming from a single source such as a window, brings out the dimension and texture on faces. There are more shadows with directional lighting. The feel of direct light can be dramatic, intense and energetic. Direct light tends to complement men well.

define relationships

An excellent way to capture a sincere aspect of personality is to photograph your subject with a person or people that he or she loves, somewhere he or she cares about or with something important to him or her. These people, places and things are intrinsically connected to the subject and will provoke unique reactions that can be caught on film and translated as tangible details to describe the person you love.

Start by listing the people, places and things that are important to your subject. The list might give you ideas on how to photograph your subject and include things that he or she holds dear. Photograph your baby with his grandparents. Take a picture of your school-aged child with her best friend or favorite teacher. Pose your husband with the family dog.

When photographing more than one subject, show the relationship between them. The subjects should be interacting in some way. Photograph a grandparent rocking a

This photo is part of a series Michelle Pendleton took to show the relationship her husband, Dwayne, shares with their twin boys, Adam (left) and Luke. To capture the dynamics of the relationship, Michelle photographed the trio while Dwayne taught the twins how to paint.

baby, friends hugging or talking, a master playing catch with his canine companion. The subjects do not have to be involved in activity, but there should be some contact.

"Taking photographs of your own family can be a tall order," says Allison Tyler Jones, professional photographer and co-author of *Designing With Photos* by Autumn Leaves, "but the payoff is worth it." Tyler Jones suggests that parents "chill out" when photographing their own family and not expect perfection. "Break through that idealized child thing," she says. "If your kid pulls the bow out of her hair, take the picture anyway."

relax the subject at the shoot

When most people see a camera pointed in their direction, they stop what they are doing and produce a cheesy smile. The goal here is to have the subject forget about the camera, drop the façade and have the personality take center stage.

Taking the time in the preparation phase will go a long way to ensure the comfort of your subject, but while you are behind the camera, don't forget to make an effort to interact with your subject to help him or her to relax further. Peek around the camera, tell jokes, talk in a funny accent, anything that will bring the subject's guard down.

"When I take pictures," Tyler Jones says, "I have the person sit down and then just talk to them. I ask them questions and see where it is that they are comfortable." Her favorite trick is to take pictures of the "in between" moments when people are more relaxed. These happen when the subjects are not expecting a photograph and therefore have their guard down.

Finally, simplify your photo to capture the essence of your subject. When looking through the viewfinder, it is easy to be engaged by the face of our subject and forget about other objects that might appear in a picture. Check the corners of the frame for distracting elements and zoom in close. If an object such as a prop doesn't add meaning to the photo, do not include it. Take vertical photos as well as horizontal shots. Change your camera's orientation until you find one that fills the frame with your subject.

Taking the time to create interpretive photos is worth it. The personality shown in these photos brings more meaning to your scrapbook pages and tells much more about the people in the pictures than a quick snapshot. ∎

step 2 | Write Heartfelt Journaling

You've overcome the first challenge in creating meaningful pages about a loved one: taking interpretive photos. Next up is to conquer the journaling. Use your feelings, the feelings of others and the perspective from your scrapbook-page subject to get to the core. Who is this person, what makes him or her tick, and why is he or she so lovable?

by Heather A. Eades

Once photos have been selected for your character-study pages, it's time to bring your subject to life through active and descriptive journaling. After reading your journaling, people should feel as if they really know and can connect with your subject. Here is a collection of information-gathering tips to help you write a concise yet emotional tribute to your loved ones.

To begin, look to the photos for inspiration. As you study them, list everything the images evoke—what do you see, feel and think about the person? Years from now, what do you want to remember about this person that you might forget if you don't write it down? What character traits jump to mind? Do those traits define this person, and if so, how and why? What are the qualities and quirks of your subject?

show, don't tell

Far too often in our journaling, we are guilty of telling the viewers what to feel instead of stirring the desired emotion within them as they read. Any successful writing models the practice of "Show, don't tell." What that means is, don't *tell* the reader "about" something. Instead, *show* the reader who the person is with imagery. For example, on "I Want to Ride My Bicycle" (p. 99), Michelle Pendleton fills her journaling with details and stories to convey the love her husband, Dwayne, has for cycling.

To show Dwayne's true love for cycling is to grab the reader's hand and take them on a bike ride with him, without ever using those words. Michelle took great care to explain how Dwayne taught his children how to ride a bike ("his gentle encouragement, steady hands and quick feet"). She paints a picture with words of the places he rides ("smoothly paved streets, trails covered in dusty pea gravel"). When composing the journaling for this page, Michelle continually challenged herself to write vividly by asking herself the following questions: Why does Dwayne love cycling? What is the feeling it gives him? How else does it play a role in his life? Where does it take him?

As you look at your photos, connect your senses with your subject. As your mind reflects upon experiences, thoughts and emotions associated with your loved one, give your reader concrete word-pictures.

use your voice

Because journaling is such an intimate element of scrapbooking, it must be done in your own voice—your own words, grammar and inflections that make the writing uniquely yours. Your language should rely on precisely chosen adjectives and adverbs focused on the main point of the character-description. Stephen King, in his book *On Writing* (Simon & Schuster), encourages writers to "use the first word that comes to your mind, if it is appropriate and colorful." He goes on to say that you can always come up with other words, but they probably won't be as good as the first ones, or as close to what you really mean. Your voice comes through in journaling when you can set yourself aside and allow your heart to pour from your pen. Write from the first thoughts that flash to mind. Your voice behind the words breathes life into your writing.

interview others

Brush up on your interviewing skills, and let the words of others expand your thoughts on your subject. Discover what senses and memories are evoked from

just **write!**

Challenge yourself to write. Set the timer for 20 minutes, and write continuously about your subject for the entire time. Here are some questions to keep your mind racing and your pen moving!

- How would you describe this person to someone who doesn't know him or her?

- Dwell on each physical feature of the person. What do you love about each part of the whole?

- What are expressions or "-isms" that are unique to this person?

- How does the person make you feel and, more important, why?

- What are the sights, smells, sounds, tastes and touches that you associate with this person? List them all.

- Who is this person to you and to those around him or her?

- What are the ordinary details about this person that make him or her so extraordinary in your life?

- What are your memories with this person, especially memories that highlight his or her characteristic traits?

- When were the photos in your layout taken and how do the photos add to the thoughts of your journaling? Are they capturing your subject in his or her element, or are they documenting a memory? Journal the information not found in the photos themselves.

- Why does this person's life make a difference in yours?

- ...And then of course, how?

another perspective. Show the photos you've chosen for your page to other family members and friends.

You may even want to discuss the photos with the subject in an interview. Michelle interviewed her husband for the "Music Soothes the Soul" layout on page 60. See the next page for a sample of her interview questions, Dwayne's responses and the resulting journaling. Try the following tips for your own interviews:

- Be prepared with your questions, and always have the appropriate tools: plenty of paper, pens or a video camera or tape recorder. You may even want to send your subject the questions ahead of time, so he or she has time to think about the answers.
- Keep your questions in chronological order, beginning with questions from the person's early years, progressing to questions about the present. This saves time when you are organizing the information.
- Try to use open-ended questions to get your subject to open up. Avoid asking simple yes or no questions, as they stray from the true essence of your subject. Remember, you are aiming to capture the heart of who he or she is. This becomes easier the more relaxed the person you're interviewing is.
- Try not to make the occasion seem too formal—have a conversation. Actively listen to your subject. He or she will be more willing to talk longer if you are enjoying yourself as well. They need to know you're interested in the things they have to share.

read, read, read

Books and magazines are another key to successful journaling. Reading quality literature helps subconsciously guide the mechanics of your writing. Studying how other authors have tackled the task of giving depth and believability to their characters also can provide inspiration for your journaling.

Charles Dickens is renowned for developing vibrant characters. Pay attention to his descriptions and word choices as he reveals Miss Havisham in *Great Expectations*. Again from Stephen King's *On Writing*, he stresses the importance of reading good writing: "You cannot hope to sweep someone else away by the force of your writing until it has been done to you."

Heartfelt journaling gives depth to those two-dimensional images in your photos. As we all strive to preserve the legacy of our lives in acid-free albums, who we were; who we are; and who we will become are all results of the impact individuals have had on us. Your heartfelt journaling is your chance to give those characters of your life the standing ovation they deserve. ∎

Turn to page 70 for design tips.

for the journaling challenged

There is no such thing as a "traditional" journaling block. Here are some fun approaches to try or to inspire journaling ideas of your own.

Conversations Write out a conversation you have had with your subject that captures the heart of your relationship or who he or she is inside. Let the dialogue speak for itself.

Lists Lists are a great way to combine your thoughts in a focused format using short sentences. Pick a theme that complements the photo(s) and go from there. Lists can be as simple as reasons why you love the person or the person's favorites. Be creative!

Letters Write a letter to the person. Share your hopes, dreams and ways you've been blessed by knowing this person all in a letter format.

Group effort Incorporate a pull-out tab element on your page, involving family members and friends. Put quotes about your subject from different people in his or her life on separate tabs that show just how special he or she is to others.

Compare and contrast Compare physical features of the person to other family members. Show how the traits of your subject are linked in your family.

Labels Labels are a great way to create a summary of your feelings while adding a visual energy to the page.

Definitions Pull out that trusty dictionary and write out the definitions of words that describe your subject, or have fun creating your own.

Memories Write out a favorite memory you have with this person as if you were telling it to someone who has never met him or her.

Mixed-media journaling There are so many papers, embellishments, stamps and stickers available that can say those words that escape you. Fill a page with simple one-word adornments that list defining words of your subject's character.

get the *story*

Try interviewing your subject, and use his or her answers for some meaty journaling. For the journaling on "Music Soothes the Soul" on page 60, Michelle Pendleton interviewed her husband, Dwayne, to help inspire the journaling. Below are some questions that Michelle asked Dwayne about music, his answers and the resulting journaling.

the interview

1. How do you feel, in detail, when you play now? "It is a very relaxing time to just pull my guitar out and play. No matter how bad or good a day I am having, playing seems to make me forget about the day and enjoy the moment. I only wish I would spend more time at it."

2. Where is your favorite place to play? "Anywhere it is quiet. The bedroom is usually my getaway place." **Time of day?** "Usually later in the evening."

3. Where would you want to play if you could choose anywhere in the world? "A beach in Hawaii." **Why?** "Why not? I have never been to a beach in Hawaii. Actually, I have never thought of playing anywhere beyond my home."

4. Who do you want to play for? "My kids, wife and friends. The ones who really matter in my life."

5. Whose music (guitar) do you admire and look up to? "Artists like (in no particular order) Richard Mullins, John Denver,

Kenny Loggins and James Taylor. **Why?** I like their sound and the sounds of an acoustic guitar."

6. How does playing affect your mood? "It lifts my spirit."

7. How do you feel after you are done playing? "Relaxed… kind of like my day is starting."

8. How does it make you feel when you share your music with your children? "Like I am a star. If they only knew I am not that good."

9. How do their reactions reflect upon your own? "It is a great feeling when my kids ask me to play for them. It makes me want to learn more and get better."

10. What part of sharing your guitar with your children will make a lasting and treasured memory? "Being at a point where I can teach them to play if they want to learn, and we could play together."

resulting journaling

"High-pitched squeals precede the virtual stampede as two toddlers scamper into my bedroom each evening. Zoe and Kyle know the bedtime routine and what special thing that will happen next. After the teeth are brushed and they are dressed in their jammies, the private concert will begin momentarily. The old, ratty black case has been retired after 20 years of use and has now been replaced with a new shiny one. The sturdy latches catch the light as it is carried out of the closet. Twenty chubby fingers eagerly try to help their father open the case. He helps guide one set of hands picking up the neck and the other with the body. Dwayne sits on the corner of the bed and the performance has begun. Before the first song could really begin, Kyle reaches into the case and pulls out a pick and thrusts it into the strong and capable hand of his father. Meanwhile, the capo sits alone in the case, and Zoe spots her opportunity to help with the concert. As the ritual has evolved, after a few songs are played, it will be time for the little ones to hone their skills. Even before he could talk, Kyle could strum the pick against the strings while his daddy played the chords. Zoe tucks her dolls into my bed as father and son play a duet. The nightly tradition is over too quickly for the little ones, but the transition into their beds is gentle. The music has slowed the inner rhythm of my active toddlers and allows them to drift into a peaceful sleep.

"What Zoe and Kyle don't know is that after their bedroom door is closed and all the goodnights have been said, Dwayne, on many nights, goes back into our bedroom and pulls that new black case from the closet. Here, with his guitar, he finds the time to center himself with the music, just as it did for our youngest set of twins moments earlier. He needs this time alone to unwind from the tension of the day. Whether he plays one song or several, I can see the tangible effects on his face and body. The muscles relax, the breathing slows, the face softens, and that smile I fell in love with many years ago returns. Some nights the other kids sneak in the room to relive the memories of bedtime concerts of not so long ago. They sit quietly at his feet, all eyes are on him, and he looks back and gives them that little smile of his and quick nod to let them know they are welcome to stay awhile. Without words, Dwayne connects with his children through music.

"I have to admit, I sneak into the concert, too. It can rejuvenate my lackluster mood when I hear sweet melodies delicately drifting through the rooms of our home. They draw me in, and I fall in love with him all over again. Dwayne, his trusty Ibanez, and a few chords make a perfect ending to a long day."

step 3 | Design With Emotion

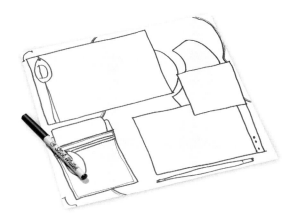

You've set the tone with the photos and captured the character with the journaling. Now it's time to design a page that enhances the emotions evoked from your images and words. Use the elements of design to help map out a complementary layout and choose mood-enhancing products.

by Heidi Schueller (Masters '03)

When designing a layout for your scrapbook, mood is an essential part of the page and can be emphasized using design elements. The five basic elements that can be used to create mood are: color, texture, linear quality, fonts and unity. As previously discussed, photos and journaling are the first elements to suggest certain emotions. However, incorporating mood with materials solidifies the suggested emotion and unifies all three page components for a successful heartfelt page. When putting together a scrapbook page, memories are re-created in a design that is focused on emotion, intoxicating the viewer with its story.

convey mood with color

Mastering this kind of emotion on a scrapbook page is easy when starting with color elements. Color targets the spirit of the layout from the beginning because it provides the artist with mood choices that will help develop the overall emotion of the page. Use the following color/mood combinations as a guide to create layouts that will generate your intended emotion:

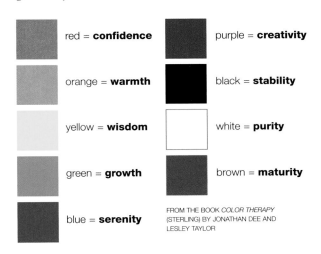

red = **confidence**

orange = **warmth**

yellow = **wisdom**

green = **growth**

blue = **serenity**

purple = **creativity**

black = **stability**

white = **purity**

brown = **maturity**

FROM THE BOOK *COLOR THERAPY* (STERLING) BY JONATHAN DEE AND LESLEY TAYLOR

Choosing the correct color scheme to complement photographic moods fuels the emotional energy necessary to apply the other four design elements to the layout.

evoke the senses with texture

When combined with the right color palette, texture stimulates a page and brings these colors to life. To exclude texture from a scrapbook page is like taking the bubbles out of champagne. Both are needed to avoid a dull and flat effect. Not only does texture create depth in a design, it also gives the opportunity to literally feel the temperament associated with the layout. Choose textures, in coordinating colors, that will enhance the mood being created, such as soft mulberry papers for baby pages, rich velvet papers for wedding pages, netting for beach pages and denim for tomboy pages. Patterned paper can influence the emotional outcome of a layout as well as textured materials. A busy pattern suggests loud texture and should be used sparingly while a soft delicate pattern can subtly entertain the entire page.

Torn cardstock or patterned paper adds character to the mood of the page because it adds texture and creates linear motion. Refer to the illustrations below to see how Michelle Pendleton used color and texture to reflect mood in her layouts.

color and texture

reflective
For "Music Soothes the Soul" (p. 60), Michelle Pendleton gravitated toward the cool tones of slate and blue to subtly spruce up a background based on organic browns and cork texture. These product choices offer a relaxed atmosphere for the reflective photos on the serene layout.

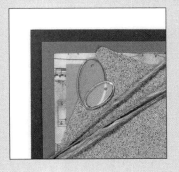

energetic
The primary colors of red, yellow and blue exude energy on "Under Construction" (p. 74). They are pure and vibrant. Michelle mixed this spirited combo with fun mesh and a red bandana to turn up the boyish energy on the resulting scrapbook page.

masculine
Michelle combined browns and other earth tones with rustic textures such as leather and industrial textures such as metal for "I Want to Ride My Bicycle" (p. 75). Natural colors and textures and industrial textures are good choices for masculine scrapbook pages.

create movement with linear quality

After choosing a color scheme and textures, linear quality needs to be incorporated into the page design. Linear quality refers to the emotional direction of a scrapbook page and is created by line and form. Soft curving lines offer subtle movement and convey a gentle emotion while hard straight lines suggest a strong and dominant movement with stable emotion.

Horizontal lines and patterns create effortless observation because the general population reads left to right allowing easy translation of page contents and emotions.

Vertical lines suggest aspiration and activity where diagonal lines create a wilder design with an energetic and dynamic feeling.

Where curvilinear, or curvaceous, lines can affect our moods by offering a relaxed natural motion on a page, rectilinear, or straight, lines create defined alert emotions because of their angles. Refer to the thumbnail sketches below left to see how Michelle use linear quality to reflect mood on her layouts.

match the theme with fonts

Fonts work in conjunction with linear quality because they also are a linear expression of mood. Typing the title for a page in a bold chunky font conveys a strong and heavy message, best used on playful and adventurous pages. Swirled, thin and romantic type fonts convey a peaceful, flowing message and are best applied on whimsical and sentimental pages.

There are three basic rules to follow when using fonts on a page. First, a font should not compete for attention on a page. Make sure it is readable and does not get lost over patterned paper or other page elements. Second, fonts can be placed just about anywhere on a layout to create movement. For example, try placing a title sideways, allowing the observer to travel around the page, absorbing its mood. Finally, choose a font style that complements the overall mood on the page.

get cohesion with unity

Mixing the above four basic elements together in one harmonious design is called unity. Even though each design element is unique, it connects with the rest through the emotion of the photographs. To achieve unity, first determine the mood of a photo. Then use each design element to reflect that emotion. For example, Michelle conveys energy and activity in every design element on her "Under Construction" layout (p. 74). The primary color scheme is bright and vibrant. She chose textures such as mesh that match the page's construction-site feel. The straight, angled lines add movement by directing the eye to and fro. Finally, the fonts' casual attitude further lends to the page's carefree feel.

Applying these four mood-evoking elements to scrapbook layouts enables the creator to suggest emotions instead of having observers guess the intended feelings. Scrapbooking is not just preserving photos in a book. It is the art of recording memories through an emotional, creative medium. Every scrapbooker benefits from learning and applying these mood-evoking elements because the finished design will not only tell a story but entertain certain feelings the observer can relate to. ∎

linear quality

reflective

To evoke a tranquil mood, Michelle Pendleton used the curved lines native to a guitar shape as the basis of her design on "Music Soothes the Soul" (p. 60). She rounded the corners of the journaling tags, used a flowing script font for the title and included round metal-rimmed tags to complete the page.

energetic

For "Under Construction" (p. 74), Michelle offset vertical lines for a design full of activity. Michelle repeated block shapes throughout the design via the photos, journaling blocks, title and accents. The off-kilter look also is symbolic of the "under construction" theme of the page.

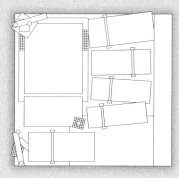

masculine

Straight, defined lines add to the masculinity of "I Want to Ride My Bicycle" (p. 75). Michelle kept the linear quality very clean and straight from the chosen fonts and the photo mats to the blocks in the patterned paper and the delicately torn edges of some of the papers, which she did for variety.

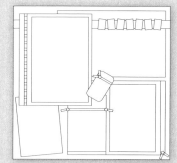

page **recipes**

Try the following page recipes to serve up just the right mood for your photos and journaling. Mix and match the suggested color schemes, textures, line qualities and fonts for your heartfelt pages.

	color	texture	line quality	font
reflective	**calming** - cool pastels cobalt blue-dominant, mint green-secondary, eggshell white-accent **peaceful** - neutrals chestnut brown-dominant, cream-secondary, taupe-accent **organic** - earth tones forest green-dominant, sandy brown-secondary, stone gray-accent	• cork • small flecked patterned paper • torn sandpaper patterned paper	• off-centered horizontal title • circle- or oval-cropped photos • soft fibers wrapped gently around tags	*Hannibal Lecter* fontface.com **Free Booter** fontconnection.com *Blackjack* fontface.com
energetic	**bright** - primary colors red-dominant, yellow-secondary, blue-accent **juicy** - saturated, fruity colors raspberry red-dominant, tangerine orange-secondary, kelly green-accent **hot** - fluorescent colors flamingo pink-dominant, lime green-secondary, sun-bleached yellow-accent	• large polka-dot patterned paper • mesh or colored screen • wide-striped patterned paper placed vertically on layout	• vertical title • adhere embellishments with foam adhesive for a "popping off the page" effect • block-cropped photos and mats	**skaterdudes** 1001freefonts.com **TO BE CONTINUED** dafont.com **dream & sugar** dafont.com
masculine	**strong** - solid/dark colors deep brick red-dominant, black-secondary, charcoal gray-accent **mature** - rustic colors tree-bark brown-dominant, taupe-secondary, forest green-accent **distinguished** - monochromatic deep royal blue-dominant, pale blue-secondary, silver-accent	• faux leather • distress flannel patterned paper by sanding it • metal studs attached vertically along photos	• thin-striped patterned paper placed horizontally on layout • rectilinear frames • geometric-shaped metal-rimmed frames	Copystruct dafont.com CORNFED dafont.com Western onescrappysite.com
romantic	**valentine** - monochromatic red-dominant, pink-secondary, white-accent **sentimental** - light and airy pastels mauve-dominant, cream-secondary, olive green-accent **passionate** - deep, saturated colors eggplant-dominant, raspberry pink-secondary, chocolate brown-accent	• machine-stitch or hand-sew some photo mats • soft rose or floral patterned paper • embossed heart patterned paper	• attach ribbons horizontally • overlay printed transparency title horizontally over an enlarged photo • add organic shapes such as flower or circle buttons	*Scriptina* onescrappysite.com *Adorable* onescrappysite.com *Fontleroy Brown* dafont.com

energetic

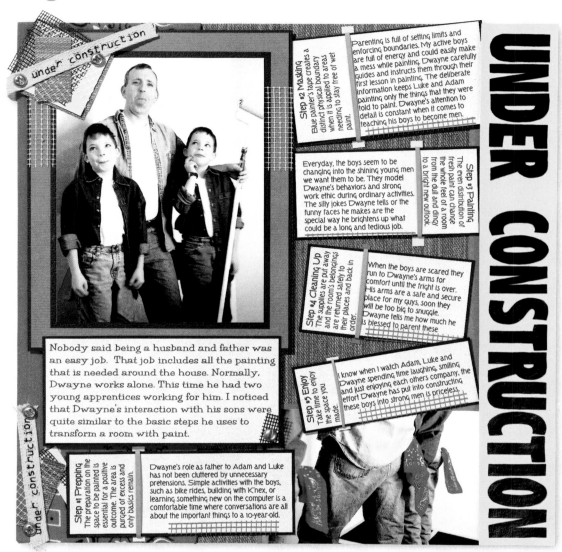

Step #2 Masking
Blue painter's tape creates a distinct physical boundary when it is applied to areas needing to stay free of wet paint.

Parenting is full of setting limits and enforcing boundaries. My active boys are full of energy and could easily make a mess while painting. Dwayne carefully guides and instructs them through their first lesson in painting. The deliberate information keeps Luke and Adam painting only the things that they were told to paint. Dwayne's attention to detail is constant when it comes to teaching his boys to become men.

Step #3 Painting
The even distribution of fresh paint can change the whole feel of a room from the dull and dingy to a bright new outlook.

Everyday, the boys seem to be changing into the shining young men we want them to be. They model Dwayne's behaviors and strong work ethic during ordinary activities. The silly jokes Dwayne tells or the funny faces he makes are the special way he brightens up what could be a long and tedious job.

Step #4 Cleaning Up
The supplies are put away and the room's belongings are returned safely to their places and back in order.

When the boys are scared they run to Dwayne's arms for comfort until the fright is over. His arms are a safe and secure place for my guys, soon they will be too big to snuggle. Dwayne tells me how much he is blessed to parent these

Nobody said being a husband and father was an easy job. That job includes all the painting that is needed around the house. Normally, Dwayne works alone. This time he had two young apprentices working for him. I noticed that Dwayne's interaction with his sons were quite similar to the basic steps he uses to transform a room with paint.

Step #5 Enjoy
Take time to enjoy the space you made.

I know when I watch Adam, Luke and Dwayne spending time laughing, smiling and just enjoying each others company, the effort Dwayne has put into constructing these boys into strong men is priceless.

Step #1 Prepping
The preparation on the space to be painted is essential for a positive outcome. The area is purged of excess and only basics remain.

Dwayne's role as father to Adam and Luke has not been cluttered by unnecessary pretensions. Simple activities with the boys, such as bike rides, building with K'nex, or learning something new on the computer is a comfortable time where conversations are all about the important things to a 10-year-old.

UNDER CONSTRUCTION

photography
To show the relationship between a father and his twin sons, Michelle Pendleton photographed her husband Dwayne while he taught the boys how to paint a room. By asking the three to interact, she was able to capture a playful yet respectful set of photos.

journaling
Michelle took a creative approach to her journaling. She likened the job of raising sons to the job of painting a room, which perfectly matches the page theme. Her journaling captions are full of imagery and detail.

design
A bright primary color scheme, angled journaling blocks, a vertical title and layered elements display activity in this layout. The textures and fonts also go hand-in-hand with the theme. This page shows movement with a dynamic design that matches the page theme.

supplies: Black paper • Red, blue and yellow papers (Club Scrap) • Patterned paper (Leisure Arts) • Twill tape (Creative Impressions) • Window screen • Drywall mesh • Red mesh (Magic Mesh) • Diamond Glaze clear gloss medium (Judikins) • Screw snaps (Making Memories) • Foam adhesive • Stamping inks • Red bandana • Tork font (1001fonts.com) • Parade font (myfonts .com) • Palent font (buyfonts.com)

masculine

I Want to Ride My

BICYCLE

Dwayne is the bike instructor, trail leader, and about as close to an extreme sports athlete that you are going to find in our house. His gentle encouragement, steady hands, and quick feet have taught each of our oldest four children to ride their first bicycles. In a few years, our youngest two will get their chance to learn to ride their own bikes, just as the older kids did, and Dwayne will be there, right along side of them, encouraging them toward independence. Until then, they eagerly climb into the orange and red bike trailer as Dad gives them a rousing ride on the streets near home.

The weekends are often filled with anticipation of where the next ride may lead. Local parks, bike paths, or the Santa Fe Trail have all been frequent destinations over the past few years for two-wheeled excursions. Proudly leading the way, Dwayne guides our children though the mazes of streets and trails to the next biking adventure.

Dwayne has glided swiftly over the smoothly paved streets, trails covered in dusty pea gravel, and once, during the off-season for skiing, he and a much more experienced biking buddy rocketed down a steep ski slope for an exhilarating and memorable mountain bike ride. The sore muscles, clothing drenched in sweat, caked on mud, and a slightly bruised ego were quickly forgotten as Dwayne dreamed of the next time he could ride his bicycle.

November 2004

photography
Dwayne Pendleton's masculinity shines because his wife, Michelle, followed basic photography guidelines: direct, natural light to complement his face; shoulders squared toward the camera, which is positioned at a lower angle; posed with a treasured object in a natural, familiar setting to relax the subject.

journaling
This journaling is a great example of "Show, don't tell." Read it to see why Dwayne loves to cycle, what it means to him and how he incorporates it into his role as a father. Michelle filled the journaling captions with precise details, vivid imagery and informative stories.

design
The neutral shades and earth tones; the block patterns, metal finishes, torn and chalked edges; the clean lines and block shapes; and the simple fonts and lettering media are the right ingredients for a masculine layout. All of the elements were deliberately chosen to complement the page theme.

supplies: Brown, tan and green papers (Bazzill) • Patterned paper (Chatterbox) • Letter stencils (Colorbök) • Leather cord • Brads (Creative Impressions) • Colorbox Fluid Chalk stamping ink (Clearsnap) • Alphabet stamps • Tag (Making Memories) • Sandpaper

It didn't take long for Angel and Alyssa to become great friends. They are so much like each other it's scary. I thought it would be fun if Lia and I took the girls shopping in San Francisco. We took bart to the city and had fun just listening to the girls talk! We had lunch at the Cheesecake Factory and shopped at numerous stores. It was a day that the girls will never forget.

friends

Amigo
Girlfriends
Playmate

Friends Gallery

Layouts that celebrate the family
we choose for ourselves.

Buddy

Chum

The Gang

Best Friend

Neighbor

Companion

Pal

Confidant

The Guys

Co-worker

Friends
Suzy West, Fremont, California

Suzy wanted to keep the photo of
these two shopping buddies the page's
focus, so she simply enlarged the image
to cover two-thirds of the layout. An
enlarged first letter for her horizontally
printed title gives the page a window-
display effect, while glimmering ribbons,
brads and a shaped clip add pizazz.

supplies: White paper • Patterned paper (BasicGrey)
• Brads (Making Memories) • Shaped clip (Making
Memories) • Ribbons

Friends Forever

Kristi Mangan
West Palm Beach, Florida

It doesn't take long for friendship to take hold, as Kristi's page illustrates through her son and his best friend. Shiny embellishments of playful words and sparkling fibers match the bright smiles of the boys. The distressed patterned tag and matting work with the labels for grounded masculinity on a happy-go-lucky, free-spirited page.

supplies: Olive and turquoise papers (Bazzill) • Patterned paper (KI Memories and Karen Foster) • Rebecca Sower Nostalgiques letter stickers (EK Success) • Twill tape (Fibers by the Yard) • Snap • Label maker (Dymo) • Wooden flowers (Li'l Davis) • Woven label (Me & My Big Ideas) • Metal word stickers (KI Memories) • Letter stamp (PSX) • Stamping ink • Zipper pull (All My Memories) • Fibers • Ribbon • Vellum • Computer font • (All following products: Making Memories) Metal-rimmed circle tag • Brads • Rub-on words and letters

Best Friend

Donna Leslie, Tinley Park, Illinois

Donna mixed elegance and playfulness together to celebrate the unique relationship she shares with her best friend. By stamping decorative images across her patterned papers, she adds fancy to the fun of scattered beads, an angled ribbon and a festive flower accent. Donna's heartfelt journaling defines what being a best friend means to her.

supplies: Patterned papers (Daisy D's and Rusty Pickle) • Ribbon • Beads (Westrim) • Mini tag • Thread • Flower • Foam stamps (Making Memories) • Brad (Making Memories) • Paint (Plaid) • Computer fonts

Jeremy

Jennifer Gallacher,
Savannah, Georgia

Jennifer was inspired to create a shadow box filled with glass pebbles from a nature frame she saw in a craft magazine. She placed her paper over foam core to create the shadow box, and then placed cut pieces of patterned papers, along with words, underneath glass pebbles within. By lifting the photo open, Jennifer reveals her love for Jeremy's many traits on individual, accented strips of paper placed neatly in stitched pockets.

supplies: Brown, red and gold papers • Foam core • Red polka-dot patterned paper (KI Memories) • Circle and square accents (KI Memories) • Map vellum (K & Co.) • Time patterned paper (Deluxe Designs) • Definition paper (Paperbilities) • Snowflake and leaf punches (Punch Bunch and Emaginations) • Letter stamps (PSX) • Stamping ink (Making Memories) • Glass pebbles (Magic Scraps) • Metal letters (Making Memories) • Eyelets (Making Memories) • Buttons (Making Memories) • Ribbon • Computer fonts

a closer look

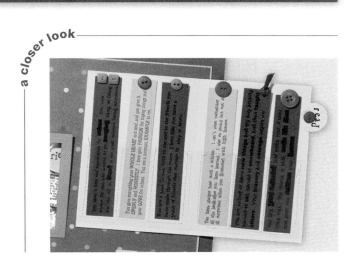

Friends

Kitty Foster, Snellville, Georgia

Those special secrets exchanged between friends are cherished on Kitty's page. The bond between her daughter and a best friend is given a timeless quality through inked papers, torn edges, inked buckles and a decoupaged zipper pull. Kitty created a textural look on this page by layering her photo over corrugated cardboard and by contrasting rough edges of paper with sleek lines in the zipper.

supplies: Ivory paper • Patterned paper (Me & My Big Ideas) • Zipper, zipper pull and buckles (Junkitz) • Fiber (Fibers By the Yard) • Brown stamping ink (Jacquard) • Foam letter stamps (Plaid) • Vintage stamping ink (Ranger) • Corrugated cardboard • Computer font

Happy Together

Cynthia Coulon, Springville, Utah

Cynthia chose plaid patterned papers and gingham ribbons to coordinate with the print in the photo and to add a hint of country charm on these 6 x 6" pages. The stitched strips of patterned paper serve as a background for whimsical word stickers. Cynthia also used walnut ink on her tags and distressed the papers and photo for a cohesive feel.

supplies: Red paper • Patterned papers (Bo-Bunny) • Tags • Transparent quotes and word stickers (Bo-Bunny) • Ribbon (Offray) • Walnut ink (Postmodern Design) • Computer fonts

RUSH!
FREE ISSUE REQUEST!

BUSINESS REPLY MAIL
FIRST-CLASS MAIL   PERMIT NO. 347   FLAGLER BEACH FL

POSTAGE WILL BE PAID BY ADDRESSEE

MEMORY
MAKERS
PO BOX 421400
PALM COAST FL   32142-7160

Meet the Girls

Emily Van Natter, Provo, Utah

Emily recorded her roommates' characteristics on this two-page spread. Each block on the layout features a close-up shot of one friend and a coordinating Disney princess. Inside jokes, qualities and quirks are all memories this fabulous six will treasure.

supplies: Blue and white papers • Patterned papers (KI Memories) • Stickers and die cuts (KI Memories, Colorbök, Making Memories, Bo-Bunny, Karen Foster, Provo Craft, Pebbles, Embossable Designs) • Rub-on letters (Making Memories) • Poemstones accents (Creative Imaginations) • Plastic charms (Doodlebug) • Label maker (Dymo) • Colored staples • Colored brads • Flower Mod Blox (KI Memories) • Safety pins • Yellow ribbon

Best Friends

Tracy Weinzapfel Burgos, Ramona, California

Tracy used muted patterns to coordinate with her sepia-toned focal photo, and then showcased close-ups of each friend in covered slide mounts. The buttons, ribbons and bows give the layout a girlish charm while the ink, stitching and torn edges add texture.

supplies: Patterned papers, decorative vellum, and die cuts (SEI) • Ribbon and bow (Queen & Co.) • Slide mounts (Loersch) • Buttons (Junkitz) • Brown stamping ink (Limited Edition) • Tag template • Computer font

Create Fun

Angela Marvel, Puyallup, Washington

Sweet, silly memories of junior high days bring back the smiles on Angela's simple design. She layered soft pastel papers, accented by a silver photo corner and ribbon, to bring out the vibrancy of her photo-machine mementos. By matting each individual pose on white and black, she brings a boldness to the page.

supplies: Dark and light lavender, black and white papers • Patterned paper (KI Memories) • Metal photo corner (Making Memories) • Rub-on words (Making Memories) • Ribbon • Computer font

Like Brothers

Audrey Lewis, Meridian, Idaho

Not only do Audrey's son and his best friend play like brothers, they tease, torment and tussle as only brothers do. Audrey documents the brotherly love between these two young friends on this layout stitched along the edges for a softer, friendly effect. She used the strip at the bottom of the page to hold stamped descriptive words. Metal brads and metal-rimmed circle tags accent the page.

supplies: Salmon, sage and dusty blue papers (SEI) • Patterned papers (Chatterbox) • Metal-rimmed circle tags • Letter stickers (EK Success) • Letter stamps (Hero Arts) • Brads (Making Memories) • Thread

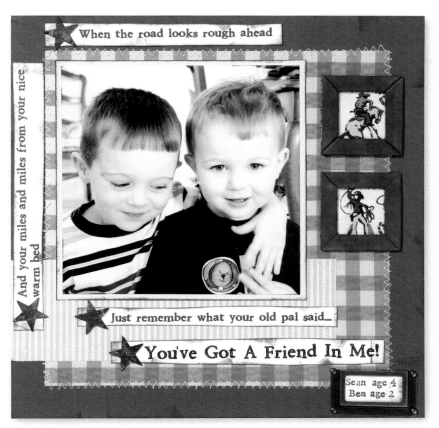

You've Got a Friend in Me

Amy L. Barrett-Arthur
Liberty Township, Ohio

Amy wanted to give this layout an old-fashioned feel so she customized the photo using image-editing software. She cut images from fabric and placed them beneath leather frames, then painted the stars with cream and black paint.

supplies: Brick red paper • Patterned papers (Daisy D's) • Letter stamps (Hero Arts) • Image-editing sotware (Adobe) • Brown stamping ink • Stars (Hobby Lobby) • Black and cream paints (Delta) • Leather frames (Making Memories) • Fabric • Metal label holder (Li'l Davis) • Brads (Lasting Impressions)

Two Is Better Than One

Susan Cyrus (Masters '04)

This computer-generated layout brings brilliant drama to the photos of Susan's son and his sidekick. She focused on the theme of "two" in everything from her son's age to the number of photos she used of the dynamic duo, and even the number of black-eyed susans on the background. Overlaying her words and numbers, using varying colors in her type and placing several elements vertically on the page makes a collage-style impact.

supplies: White paper • Image-editing software (Adobe) • Computer fonts

Best Friends

Jen Nichols, Orland, Indiana

Jen created this page for the best friend she's had since elementary school. She trimmed metal mesh with wire cutters to mat her photo and then adhered it to the page using washers and brads. Jen wrapped soft purple ribbon around the brads for texture and color.

supplies: Sage and purple papers • Patterned papers (K & Co.) • Stickers (Colorbök, Creative Imaginations) • Wire mesh and washers • Ribbon (Offray) • Sage brads (Jo-Ann) • Clear gloss medium • Transparency • Computer font

Us Two

Cheryl Manz, Paulding, Ohio

Cheryl designed this page to demonstrate how two friends complete each other. By distressing with paints and inks and adding collaged blocks to the spread, she sets a shabby-chic scene for her photos. Cheryl's journaling explains the two friends' contrasting qualities.

supplies: Kraft paper • Patterned paper (KI Memories, MOD and Chatterbox) • Word stickers (Chatterbox, Bo-Bunny and Pebbles) • Epoxy words (Creative Imaginations) • Letter stickers (Creative Imaginations, Chatterbox and Me & My Big Ideas) • Acrylic accent (KI Memories) • Stamping ink • Ribbon (May Arts) • "Inspire" woven label (Me & My Big Ideas) • Acrylic paint • Staples

Enduring Friendship

Shelley Rankin, Fredericton, New Brunswick, Canada

The silliness, funny faces and fully supportive embraces shared between best friends are captured here in an expressive collage. Shelley's son and his friend just love to laugh together, and she let them ham it up when taking their photos. A large negative strip along the right conceals her journaling and adds an animated element to the design, accented by word stickers, printed vellum and dimensional details.

supplies: Patterned paper (K & Co.) • Printed vellum (Scrapbook Sally and Dèjá Views by C-Thru Ruler) • Letter stencil (Autumn Leaves) • Rub-on phrases (Royal) • Negative strip (Creative Imaginations) • Page pebbles (Making Memories) • Letter stickers (EK Success) • Stickers (Sweetwater)

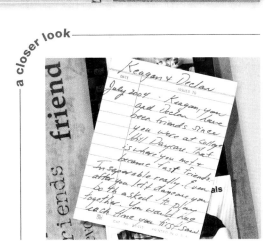

a closer look

open

Carol and Amy

Amy Goldstein, Kent Lakes, New York

What began as shared trips to the grocery store for milk and toilet paper sparked a spirit of adventure in these two buddies. Amy created this shopping-bag page to document the greatest part of their now infamous shopping expeditions—the friendship. The view above shows the two hinged doors on the page open.

---

supplies: Patterned papers (Scrapworks) • Printed circles and conchos (Scrapworks) • Round metal label holder (Li'l Davis) • Printed ribbon (Creative Impressions) • Escutcheon (EK Success) • Mailbox letters (Making Memories) • Tissue and bag handles • Hinges • Computer fonts

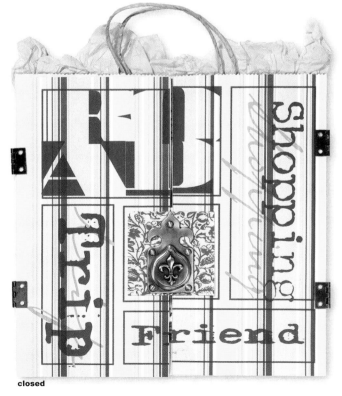

closed

Girlfriends

Melissa Diekema
Grand Rapids, Michigan

The friendship this trio established over the preschool year is evident in the close-up focal photo and is expanded on in the filmstrip shots. Melissa pulled the colors used on the page from the striped shirt in the photos.

supplies: Light blue and cream papers • Patterned paper (KI Memories) • Sketch Letter stamps (Fontwerks) • Distress ink (Ranger) • Ribbon (Stampin' Up) • Heart slide (Leave Memories) • Negative strip (Creative Imaginations) • Definitions and blossom (Making Memories) • Colored brads (Happy Hammer) • Label maker (Dymo) • Computer font

Friends

Shannon Watt, Newhall, California

Shannon played up the girls' fashion sense on the page, using ribbons and bows. The black polka-dot ribbon brings definition and Hepburn-style class. Shannon stapled ribbons onto her photo mat and painted the page edges in random thicknesses.

supplies: Lime and white papers • Patterned papers (Creative Imaginations) • Letter stickers (Creative Imaginations, American Crafts) • Punch-outs (KI Memories) • Label sticker (Pebbles) • Flower (K & Co.) • Frame (Making Memories) • Date stamp (Making Memories) • Brad (Making Memories) • Flower stamp • Ribbons • Stamping ink • Black paint (Delta) • Staples • Computer font

A Newfound Friendship

Cari Locken, Edmonton, Alberta, Canada

The kindness exchanged between children lights up this page with its simple message. Cari emphasized the lines in the photos—horizontal siding and vertical trees—and duplicated them in striped borders. Leaving negative spaces for her title blocks makes a powerful contrast with the photos' softer shades.

supplies: Black, blue, olive and cream papers • Patterned paper (Chatterbox) • Rub-on letters (Making Memories) • Letter stickers (Creative Imaginations; Rebecca Sower Nostalgiques and Sticko by EK Success) • Black stamping ink • Flea Market font (twopeasinabucket.com)

ABCs of Friendship

Melodee Langworthy, Rockford, Michigan

Melodee made this page with a distressed and vintage look to capture the rugged heart of boyhood best buddies. She added her own custom components by scanning a blank library card, typing in her journaling in image-editing software, and then printing it onto a transparency. She adhered the transparency to matching patterned paper and tucked it behind the smaller photo. She also played up the stitched print on the paper by stitching with black thread around the page.

supplies: Patterned papers (7 Gypsies and Karen Foster) • Die-cut letters (Foofala) • Die-cut frame and words (This That) • Letter stamps (EK Success) • Library card • Transparency • Black thread • Black stamping ink • Chalk ink (Clearsnap) • Computer font

Bosom Buddies

Denine Zielinski, Nanticoke, Pennsylvania

A second generation of friendship shines through on Denine's page, highlighting the bond between her best friend's child and her own son. She chose bright and energetic patterned paper to capture the moment of the photo, and painted her stencil letters to coordinate. She stitched the top and bottom of the layout for a heartwarming touch and tied off accents of colorful fabric strips through red eyelets.

supplies: Red and olive papers (Bazzill) • Striped patterned papers (Daisy D's) • Letter stickers (KI Memories) • Red eyelets • Fabric strips • Punched metal letters (Colorbök) • Letter charm (Making Memories) • Acrylic paint (Making Memories) • Thread

New Friends

Danielle Thompson, Tucker, Georgia

Danielle captured the colors and energy of being outside through her cheerful color scheme and playful embellishments. She sanded the edges of her photos, stamped her journaling block and framed small photos with handmade "slide mounts." By printing two photos in monotones of red and green, she ties the two pages together.

supplies: Red, white and sage papers • Patterned papers (KI Memories) • Letter stamps (Hero Arts, Educational Insights and Making Memories) • Rickrack (Wrights) • Flower punch (EK Success) • Button-Up accents (EK Success) • Rub-on words (Making Memories) • Tattoos rub-ons (KI Memories) • Stamping ink

July 2004

Lauren

Kim

When Lauren and Kim were four years old, Kim's family moved into the house next door to Lauren. They became friends instantly, attending the same school, playing and swimming at each other's homes. It wasn't until they became older and started playing matchmaker with the help of Stephanie, Lauren's younger sister that they became family. The three of them were swapping phone numbers between Julie, Lauren and Stephanie's oldest sister and Gabriel, Kim's older brother. Although the girls exaggerated the truth a bit, a true love story was born and on April 17, 2004, Julie and Gabriel were married. The girls knew all along that they were meant to be family.

Neighbors first   **Friends** second   **Family** at last

Neighbors, Friends, Family
Kathy Lewis, Temple City, California

When boy-next-door married girl-next-door, these two best friends finally became the "sisters" they always knew they were meant to be. Kathy documented the transformation of the two girls' relationship from friends to family on this bright and sunny friendship layout, accented by a wedding tag of their now-married brother and sister. Kathy furthered the depth of this page by applying a mixture of green acrylic paint and white dimensional paint over the fern stencil, and then rubbed a white craft pad over the images to add highlights.

supplies: Yellow, cream and sage papers (Bazzill) • Patterned papers, patterned vellum and rivets (Chatterbox) • Fibers (Fibers by the Yard) • Metal label holders (Jo-Ann) • Fern plastic stencil (Delta) • Dimensional paint (Delta) • Silk flower • Date stamp • Brads • Metal-rimmed circle tag and jump ring • Green acrylic paint • White craft ink pad • Kedzie Lite DNA and Angelina fonts (downloaded from the Internet)

Smiles That Are Contagious

Suzy West, Fremont, California

When Suzy's friends start smiling, all one can do is sit back and join in. Suzy combined energetic patterns in her papers and secured her photo mat in place with a belt buckle accent. She used large foam stamps to create the word "contagious" in her title, expanding it across the page. Antiqued brads and inked twill tape lend definition and unifying accents to this light-hearted page.

supplies: Patterned papers (Chatterbox) • Rub-on title letters (Making Memories) • Lock charm (All My Memories) • Jump ring • Brads • Printed twill tape (All My Memories) • Transparency • Foam letter stamps (Making Memories) • Paint (Delta) • Buckle

Little Girls

Michelle Tornay
Newark, California

Michelle created this feminine, pastel layout to embrace the friendship between these cousins. Michelle never would have guessed that her sister's daughter would become her own daughter's best friend. She highlights their similarities here in photos and journaling. She painted and stitched the edges of the photos to meld with the patterned paper, and then painted her paper and rub-on words to complement the color scheme.

supplies: Periwinkle paper • Patterned paper (Autumn Leaves) • Printed twill (7 Gypsies) • Brads (Making Memories) • Rub-on words (Making Memories) • Photo turns (7 Gypsies) • Transparency • Paint • Stamping ink • Flea Market font (twopeasinabucket.com) • Silk flowers

Shared Joy

Carrie Colbert, The Woodlands, Texas

Bright and bubbly, Carrie's simple yet festive layout celebrates the camara-derie between her and her closest friends. Carrie had thrown a special party for her support system of smiling faces, showcased here on this jovial, geometric design. Her journaling is tucked inside the corner vellum envelope.

supplies: Yellow and red papers • Circle and striped patterned papers (SEI) • Metal-rimmed tag • Square page pebbles • Vellum envelope • Computer fonts

Xtreme Friends

Barb Hogan, Cincinnati, Ohio

Layers of torn paper make Barb's design swoosh around the page. Bright-colored strips of paper behind the matted photo act as skis. She carried the "xtreme" theme through her design, embossing the torn paper "x" in the title, stitching an assortment of "x's" and smudging black ink on both the papers and photo for a blustery effect. Barb journaled the highlights of this frosty occasion by printing on a transparency.

supplies: Black, red and yellow papers (Bazzill) • Patterned papers (7 Gypsies and Mustard Moon) • Fibers • Embossing powder • Letter stickers (Wordsworth) • Stamping ink (Stampin' Up) • Transparency (Avery) • Amazon font (downloaded from the Internet) • Jack Frost font (twopeasinabucket.com)

Cedar Street Gang

Pam Easley, Bentonia, Mississippi

To bring new life to old friendships, Pam scanned an old, faded Polaroid print and then corrected the contrast and removed scratches using image-editing software. She printed the new and improved photo of her childhood chums to look like a large Polaroid. The vibrant colors and pop-art patterns immerse the page in '60s style while shiny, decorative paper clips accessorize the design.

supplies: Orange paper (Bazzill) • Patterned paper (KI Memories) • Shaped clips (7 Gypsies) • Transparency • Computer fonts

Girlfriends Rock

Kelly Surace
Baton Rouge, Louisiana

What began as a slumber party ended up in an impromptu photo-shoot for Kelly's sister and her friends. The results are displayed on this computer generated page as a celebration of the amazing friendship among the four girls. Kelly wanted the girls to remember that no matter where they go or what they do, they will always have each other.

supplies: Image-editing software (Adobe) • Computer fonts

Create-&-Trade Album

Celebrate friendships by creating and then trading pages for a theme album.

For a fun way to connect with a group of friends, make a create-and-trade album. There are several ways you can facilitate this project. Creating a page for each friend and then trading pages at your next get-together is one way. Or, do what this group did—pair up friends to do a page about one another but make multiples so each group member has an original page for her album.

The six girlfriends who created this colorful 8 x 8" album met on an online scrapbooking site. They suggest you choose a common color palette before you begin. They selected the brightly colored purse patterned fabric album by We R Memory Keepers (shown above) first then each member chose a color palette to complement it.

Making these pages showcased their talents, celebrated friendships and offered each other a snapshot of their lives. They learned a lot about one another from the journaling-inspiring interviews they held.

Stacy Yoder of Yucaipa, California, journaled on an array of tags to reveal fun facts about fellow crop friend, Jen, such as her favorite show and favorite drink. Stacy accented the tags with colorful ribbons and buttons.. A wavy machine stitch connects color-blocked papers to create the background.

supplies: Pink paper (Bazzill) • Blue patterned paper (Making Memories) • Green patterned paper (Chatterbox) • Patterned vellum (SEI) • Tags (Chatterbox) • Clear buckle and ribbon with words (Junkitz) • Ribbon and eyelets (Making Memories) • Jolee's flowers (EK Success) • Buttons • CAC One Seventy font (scrapvillage.com)

Jennifer Bourgeault (Masters '04) included basic statistics about her online friend on this page. She also added a sentiment about when the two first met in person. Jennifer accented the focal photo with circles that spell Stacy's name. A label holder corals colorful buttons that tie the circles into the page.

supplies: White, green, purple and pink papers • Circle punch (Marvy) • Letter stickers (Li'l Davis, Creative Imaginations, Making Memories, Me & My Big Ideas) • Button letters and buttons (Junkitz) • Label holder (Magic Scraps) • Black stamping ink • Flamenco Font (scrapvillage.com)

Birthdate: June 5, 1971 • Age: 33 • Hometown: Yucaipa, California • Married to Steve for 14 years • Children: Josh (12), Lauren (8) and Rebecca (3) • Homeschooler • Reality TV Junkie • Self-proclaimed "homebody" • Fave foods: Ice Cream and Pizza

I was so excited when I got to actually meet Stacy on our journey to Junkitz! She is such a sweetheart both online and IRL!

Amy Warren of Tyler, Texas, used straight and curved edges to add motion to this page. To make the wavy bottom border, she adhered patterned paper onto a slightly larger piece of brown paper. To create the title, she stamped letters on yellow paper strips with paint. Strips of fabric threaded through punched holes add dimension.

supplies: Brown and yellow papers • Patterned papers (Basicgrey) • Foam alphabet stamps (Making Memories) • White paint (Delta) • Fabric strips • Brown stamping ink • Rivets (Chatterbox) • Computer font • Bluecake font (onescrappysite.com)

Using brown thread, Julie Medeiros of South Jordan, Utah, stitched around the edges of the background, mat and triangle to add definition. She painted, sanded and inked the "a"—a puzzle piece. Then Julie adhered strips of patterned paper to the negative portion of the puzzle and inked the edges. Metal letters spell out "Amy."

supplies: Green, blue, orange and pink papers (Bazzill) • Patterned paper (Paper Fever) • Puzzle piece letter and metal letters (Making Memories) • White paint (Delta) • Nick Bantock Van Dyke Brown stamping ink (Ranger)

Teri Anderson of Idaho Falls, Idaho, sewed the edges of the background then randomly adhered patterned paper strips to create a lively border on this page. A spiral clip dangling on a polka-dot ribbon lures the eye to the focal photo. Patterned paper and pink paper strips stamped with text accent the tags .

supplies: Patterned papers (SEI, Paper Love) • Tags • Ribbon (SEI) • Alphabet stamps (PSX) • Letter stickers (SEI, Wordsworth) • Black stamping ink • Fluid Chalk Charcoal Ink (Clearsnap) • Spiral clip (7 Gypsies)

Bright colored tags and ribbons pop against the black background on this page by Jennifer Bertsch of Tallahassee, Florida. Jennifer tore the top edge of a mini envelope for a pocket and then layered it with a square piece of chipboard and patterned paper for dimension. Button and flower accents hint to the subject's playful personality.

supplies: Black paper (Bazzill) • Patterned paper (KI Memories) • Chipboard square (Bazzill) • Alphabet stamps (EK Success) • Tags (SEI, Li'l Davis) • Ribbon (Offray) • Flower and circle punches • Mini envelope • Buttons

product guide

The following companies manufacture the products featured in this book.
Check your local scrapbook retailer or arts-and-crafts store to find the products.

7 Gypsies
480-325-3358 7gypsies.com

Adobe™
adobe.com

All My Memories
888-553-1998 allmymemories.com

American Crafts
800-879-5185 americancrafts.com
(wholesale only)

American Tag Company
800-223-3956 americantag.net

Ampersand Art Supply
ampersandart.com

Anna Griffin, Inc.
888-817-8170 annagriffin.com
(wholesale only)

Artistic Expressions
artisticexpressionsinc.com

Autumn Leaves
800-588-6707

Avery® Dennison
averydennison.com

BasicGrey
basicgrey.com

Bazzill Basics Paper
480-558-8557 bazzillbasics.com

Blumenthal Lansing Co.
563-538-4211 buttonsplus.com

Bo-Bunny Press
801-771-4010 bobunny.com

Boxer Scrapbook Productions
503-625-0455
boxerscrapbooks.com

Canson, Inc.®
800-628-9283
canson-us.com

Card Connection
cardconnection.com

Carolee's Creations®
435-563-1100 ccpaper.com

Chatterbox, Inc.
208-939-9133 chatterboxinc.com

Clearsnap®, Inc.
800-448-4862 clearsnap.com
(wholesale only)

Close To My Heart
888-655-6552 closetomyheart.com

Club Scrap™, Inc.
888-634-9100 clubscrap.com

Coats & Clark
800-648-1479 coatsandclark.com

Colorbök™, Inc.
800-366-4660 colorbok.com
(wholesale only)

Craf-T Products
507-236-3996 craftproducts.com

Creative Imaginations
800-942-6487 cigift.com
(wholesale only)

Creative Impressions
719-596-4860
creativeimpressions.com

Creative Memories
800-468-9335
creative-memories.com

C-Thru® Ruler Company, The
800-243-8419 cthruruler.com
(wholesale only)

Daisy D's Paper Company
888-601-8955 daisydspaper.com

Dan River, Inc.
danriver.com

DecoArt
decoart.com

Delta Technical Coatings, Inc.
800-423-4135 deltacrafts.com

Deluxe Designs™
480-497-9005 deluxecuts.com

Die Cuts With a View™
801-224-6766
diecutswithaview.com

DMC Corporation
973-589-0606
dmc-usa.com

DMD Industries, Inc.
800-805-9890 dmdind.com
(wholesale only)

Doodlebug Design™
801-966-9952
timelessmemories.ca

Dritz
dritz.com (wholesale only)

Duncan Enterprises
800-438-6226
duncan-enterprises.com

Dymo
dymo.com

Educational Insights
edin.com

EK Success™, Ltd.
800-524-1349 eksuccess.com
(wholesale only)

Emagination Crafts, Inc.
630-833-9521
emaginationcrafts.com
(wholesale only)

Embellish It
720-312-1628 embellishit.com

Fibers By The Yard
800-760-8901 fibersbytheyard.com

Flair Designs
888-546-9990 flairdesignsinc.com

Flax Art & Design
flaxart.com

Flights of Fancy
flightsoffancyboutique.com

Font Werks
fontwerks.com

Foofala
402-330-3208 foofala.com

Grumbacher
grumbacherart.com

Hammermill
hammermill.com

Hap's Memories
hapsmemories.com

Happy Hammer, The
303-690-3883
thehappyhammer.com

Hirschberg Schultz & Co.
800-221-8640 (wholesale only)

Hero Arts® Rubber Stamps, Inc.
800-822-4376 heroarts.com
(wholesale only)

Hill Creek Designs
619-562-5799 hillcreekdesigns.com

Hobby Lobby
hobbylobby.com

Hot Off The Press, Inc.
800-227-9595 craftpizazz.com

Impress Rubber Stamps
206-901-9101
impressrubberstamps.com

Inkadinkado® Rubber Stamps
800-888-4652 inkadinkado.com

Jacquard Products
800-442-0455
jacquardproducts.com

JewelCraft, LLC
201-223-0804 jewelcraft.biz

JHB International
800-525-9007

Jo-Ann Fabrics
joannfabrics.com

JudiKins
310-515-5115
judikins.com

Junkitz
junkitz.com

K & B Innovations
shrinkydinks.com

K & Company
888-244-2083 kandcompany.com

Karen Foster Design™
801-451-9779
karenfosterdesign.com
(wholesale only)

KI Memories
972-243-5595 kimemories.com

Krylon
800-4KRYLON

Lasting Impressions for Paper, Inc.
800-9-EMBOSS

Leave Memories
leavememories.com

Leisure Arts
800-643-8030
leisurearts.com

Li'l Davis Designs
949-838-0344 lildavisdesigns.com

Limited Edition Rubber Stamps
650-594-4242
LimitedEditionRS.com

Liquitex®
888-4ACRYLIC liquitex.com

Loersch
loersch.com

Ma Vinci's Reliquary
crafts.dm.net/mall/reliquary

Magic Mesh, The
magicmesh.com

Magic Scraps™
972-238-1838
magicscraps.com

Making Memories
800-286-5263
makingmemories.com

Marvy® Uchida
800-541-5877 uchida.com
(wholesale only)

May Arts
mayarts.com (wholesale only)

Maya Road
mayaroad.com

Me & My Big Ideas
949-583-2065
meandmybigideas.com
(wholesale only)

Michael Miller Memories
michaelmillermemories.com

Michaels® Arts & Crafts
800-542-4235 michaels.com

Microsoft
microsoft.com

Milliken & Company
milliken.com

MOD My Own Design
303-641-8680
mod-myowndesign.com

Mustard Moon™ Paper Co.
408-229-8542 mustardmoon.com

My Mind's Eye, Inc.
801-298-3709
frame-ups.com

National Cardstock
866-452-7120

National Paper & Packaging
nationalpaper.com

Nature's Pressed
800-850-2499
naturespressed.com

NRN Designs
nrndesigns.com

Nunn Design
nunndesign.com

Offray & Son, Inc.
offray.com

On the Surface
847-675-2520

Once Upon A Scribble
onceuponascribble.com

Outdoors and More
outdoorsandmore.com

Paper Adventures
800-727-0699
paperadventures.com
(wholesale only)

Paper Company, The
800-426-8989 thepaperco.com

Paperfever
800-477-0902 paperfever.com

Paper Garden, The
435-867-6398
mypapergarden.com
(wholesale only)

Paper House Productions
paperhouseproductions.com

Paper Loft, The
801-254-1961 paperloft.com
(wholesale only)

Pebbles, Inc.
pebblesinc.com

Plaid Enterprises, Inc.
800-842-4197 plaidonline.com

Postmodern Design
405-321-3176

Provo Craft®
888-577-3545 provocraft.com
(wholesale only)

PSX Design™
800-782-6748 psxdesign.com

Punch Bunch
254-791-4209
punchbunch.com

Queen & Co.
queenandco.com

QuicKutz®
888-702-1146 quickutz.com

Ranger Industries, Inc.
800-244-2211 rangerink.com

Renaissance Art Stamps
860-567-2785

River City Rubber Works
877-735-BARN
rivercityrubberworks.com

Rusty Pickle, The
801-274-9588 rustypickle.com

Sakura of America
800-776-6257 gellyroll.com

Sakura Hobby Craft
310-212-7878 sakuracraft.com

Scrapworks, LLC
scrapworks.com

SEI, Inc.
800-333-3279 shopsei.com

Shrinky Dinks
shrinkydinks.com

Simon & Schuster, Inc.
simonsays.com

Stampers Anonymous
440-333-7941

Stampendous!®
800-869-0474 stampendous.com

Stampin' Up!®
800-782-6787 stampinup.com

Stamps Happen, Inc.
stampshappen.com

Staples
staples.com

Sweetwater Scrapbook Stickers & Papers
800-359-3094
sweetwaterscrapbooks.com

Target
target.com

Timeless Touches
623-362-8285 timelesstouches.net

Tsukineko®, Inc.
800-769-6633 tsukineko.com

Wal-Mart
walmart.com

Walnut Hollow® Farm, Inc.
800-950-5101
(wholesale only)

Westrim/Memories Forever
800-727-2727 westrimcrafts.com

Winsor & Newton
winsornewton.com

Wordsworth Stamps
719-282-3495
wordsworthstamps.com

Wrights® Ribbon Accents
877-597-4448

YLI
ylicorp.com

We have made every attempt to properly credit the items mentioned in this book. If any company has been listed incorrectly, please contact Darlene D'Agostino at darlene.dagostino@fwpubs.com.

resources | product guide

family & friends scrapbook pages